Julia Nuriakhmetova

Cognitive research phraseology

Julia Nuriakhmetova

Cognitive research phraseology

Functional and cognitive potential of English verb-name phraseomatic word combinations

ScienciaScripts

Imprint

Any brand names and product names mentioned in this book are subject to trademark, brand or patent protection and are trademarks or registered trademarks of their respective holders. The use of brand names, product names, common names, trade names, product descriptions etc. even without a particular marking in this work is in no way to be construed to mean that such names may be regarded as unrestricted in respect of trademark and brand protection legislation and could thus be used by anyone.

Cover image: www.ingimage.com

This book is a translation from the original published under ISBN 978-3-8433-1516-6.

Publisher:
Sciencia Scripts
is a trademark of
International Book Market Service Ltd., member of OmniScriptum Publishing Group
17 Meldrum Street, Beau Bassin 71504, Mauritius
Printed at: see last page
ISBN: 978-620-2-97689-3

Copyright © Julia Nuriakhmetova
Copyright © 2021 International Book Market Service Ltd., member of OmniScriptum Publishing Group

Contents

Introduction

The complexity of the problem of phraseomatic meaning and its conceptual organization can be mainly explained by the fact that the boundary between free word combinations and phraseological units is not clearly defined. The so-called *free phrases are* only relatively free, since the compatibility of words-components is strongly limited by their lexical and grammatical valence, which makes at least many of them very close to *stable combinations*. There are countless intermediate cases between the extremes of full motivation and the variety of words-components and the lack of motivation combined with full stability of lexical components and grammatical structure (Ginzburg 1966).

In this paper a new perspective of consideration of the phaseomatic value - cognitive. In recent years, the category of unit value has received a new interpretation in actively developing cognitive linguistics. The use of its scientific apparatus and the development of a special methodology to study the conceptual organization and functioning of phraseomatic phrases in various aspects seems extremely promising.

The research was based on the data from the Longman Dictionary of Contemporary English (LDCE). The total fund of the analyzed English verb-name phraseological phrases is over 2000 units.

Целью данного исследования является реконструкция концептуальной организации фразеоматического значения на примере английских глагольно-именных фразеоматических сочетаний. В свою очередь выявление концептуальной организации служит этапом в определении функционально-cognitive potential of the language units under consideration.

Theoretical basis for this dissertation was provided by the works of different researchers: in the field of cognitive linguistics - E.S. Kubryakova, V.Z. Demiankova, Z.D. Popova, I.A. Sternina, Lakoffa J.; in the field of phraseology and, in particular, phraseomatics - A. V. Kunina, N. N. Amosova, V. Vinogradov, V. L. Dashevskaya, L. A. Uralova, V. M. Kalimullina, A. F. Batyrova, and M. A. Grosheva;

The method of reconstruction of the conceptual organization is based on on onomasiological interpretation of definitions of phraseomatic combinations, according to which verb units identify the concept, and other words and labels identify the features of this concept.

This paper consists of an introduction, two chapters, a conclusion and a list of used literature and dictionaries.

The first chapter **"Theoretical prerequisites for studying the conceptual organization of the meaning of phraseomatic word combinations"** gives an overview of the linguistic literature on issues related to the development and current state of phraseology, defines the theoretical prerequisites of the cognitive perspective of the study of phraseomatic combinations, as well as the definition, classification and description of their structure and semantics.

The second chapter, **"Conceptual organization of the meanings of the English verb-name phraseomatic word combinations in the English explanatory dictionary"**, explores the functional and cognitive potential of the English verb-name phraseomatic units on the basis of a preliminary analysis of their conceptual structures, reconstructed using onomasiological interpretation of these definitions.

In conclusion, the results of the research are summarized and the conclusions of the analysis are formulated.

The list of literature and dictionaries represents literary and lexicographical sources used in the study.

Chapter I **Theoretical prerequisites for studying the conceptual organization of the meaning of phraseological phrases**

§ 1 Phraseological units as an object of linguistic

1.1. Main problems of phraseology and their solution

The phraseology of any language is the most valuable linguistic heritage, which reflects the vision of the world, national culture, customs and beliefs, fantasy and history of the people who speak it (Cherdantseva 1996).

Among linguists there is no unity on many important issues. These are semantic properties of phraseology, translatability of phraseological units. The complexity of phraseology is not only in the multi-valued interpretation of the term itself. It is conditioned by the contradictory nature of its units: being language units, at the same time they seem to go beyond the limits of language resources, by their methods of formation and linguistic designation of phenomena and objects of surrounding reality (Alekhine 1979).

As for the scope of phraseology, there are contradictory points of view depending on the understanding of the phraseological unit: M.I. Fomina believes that the object of phraseology as a science are phraseologists, which are characterized by a full set of basic distinguishing categorical features. They will become more obvious if a complex diverse phraseological unit is compared with a word on the one hand and a word combination on the other (Fomina 1983).

Unlike a word with its constant integrity (in terms of composition of sounds and morphemes) and unidirectionality, phraseology is characterized by lexical and accentological separation. The lexical meaning of each word is separate. It refers to an object, concept, action, etc. The meaning of phraseology is always expressive. It is not free, semantically indivisible, because it is completely or partially unmotivated meaning of the components of words, which are no longer called words, but components, thus emphasizing their full or partial lexical emptiness, desemanticization. This value is called phraseological.

Thus, one of the main categorical and essential features of phraseology is the presence of expressive, holistic phraseological meaning.

There are similarities between a word and a phraseological unit. It consists in the fact that both units are perceived as ready-made; each word and each phraseology is characterized by regular correlations with the same part of speech, i.e., they perform similar syntactic functions.

Many Russian linguists define a phraseological unit differently, calling it phraseology, stable word combination, phraseology, etc..

V.P. Zhukov considers phraseology to be a stable and reproducible separately formed unit of language, consisting of components, endowed with integral (or less often partially integral) meaning and combined with other words. He notes that phraseology begins where the semantic realization of its components ends (Zhukov 1978).

N.M. Shanskiy believes that a phraseological turn is a ready-made unit of two or more percussive components of verbal character, fixed in value, composition and structure (Shanskiy 1972).

There are many other definitions of a phraseological unit and all are similar in that they recognize it as a sustainable entity, although sustainability is understood differently. A.V. Kunin distinguishes the following types of stability of a phraseological unit:

1) Sustainability of use, that is, the fact that phraseology is a unit of language, not an individual education. An indicator of this type of micro-resistance is reproduction in the finished form;

2) структурно-семантическая устойчивость, т.е. фразеологическая единица состоит из не менее чем двух слов, является раздельнооформленным образованием и не обладает типовым значением, т.е. не может служить образцом для создания аналогичных фразеологических единиц по структурносемантиc model;

3) Semantic stability is manifested in the fact that for all norms and occazional structural and lexical changes of a phraseological unit, all its variants have some semantic and lexical invariant;

4) lexical stability, i.e., complete inexchangeability of components or the possibility of normative replacement of components only within the phraseological variability (Kunin 1974).

A.V. Kunin concludes that the stability of a phraseological unit is a volume of different types of microstability inherent in it. Accordingly, he defines a phraseological unit as a stable combination of lexemes with a fully or partially rethought value. This definition of a phraseological unit is accepted by many linguists as working unit and is used by them as a starting point in development of the theory of phraseology.

1.2. Phraseology: its limits and volume

Phraseology is the science of phraseological units, i.e., stable combinations of words with complicated semantics, not formed by generating structurally semantic models of variable combinations (Kunin 1986).

The term "phraseology" has two definitions: the section of linguistics, which studies the phraseological composition of language in its modern state and historical development; the set of phraseologisms of this language (Yartseva 1990).

The subject of phraseology as a section of linguistics is the study of the nature of phraseologies and their categorical features and identification of patterns of their functioning in speech.

Phraseology is an extremely complex phenomenon; its study requires its method of research and the use of other sciences - lexicology, grammar, stylistics, phonetics, history of linguistics, history, philosophy, logic and country studies. Phraseology studies the specificity of phraseology as a sign of secondary education, in particular - as a product of a special type of secondary nomination - indirect, represented by various kinds of syntagmatic interaction of words-components in the processes of rethinking and formation of a new meaning of the original combination or a single word. Phraseology also studies the peculiarities of the sign function of phraseologisms, their meaning, structural and semantic specificity manifested in the main features of phraseology - stability and reproducibility, explores the nature of the components of phraseologisms, their syntactic and morphological structure, the nature of syntactic relationships with other units of language and forms of implementation in speech, the nature of restrictions in the modifications possible for free analogues of phraseology. A special task of phraseology is to study the system of relations both between idioms and between idioms and general linguistic system of significant units - mainly words.

Исследуется специфика functionally stylistic дифференциации фразеологизмов и соотношения нейтральных для языка лексических способов номинации и экспрессивно окрашенных наименований фразеологического характера. Одной из задач фразеологии также является изучение процессов фразообразования в их номинативном и коммуникативно-functional aspects, and description of phraseological derivation - the formation of new meanings of words based on the values of phraseology.

Phraseology develops principles for identifying phraseological units, methods of their study, classification and description in dictionaries.

Phrazeology is associated with history and literature studies, not primarily with linguistic disciplines: lexicology, semantics, grammar, phonetics, stylistics, history of language and linguistics. Phaseological units consist of words, and the word is the main subject of lexicology. The theory of lexical meaning, developed in semantics, helps to reveal the semantic features of phraseological units and determine the different types of phraseological meaning. Morphology helps to understand what is lost and what is omitted deliberately, because a word in a phraseological unit does not always lose its morphological features. Syntax is important in determining the grammatical features of phraseological units, their grammatical structure and function. Phonetics determines the different pronunciation of a word in a phraseological unit. The phraseological stylistics, studying stylistic possibilities of phraseological units, is based on the experience of lexical stylistics. History of language and etymology are necessary for etymological analysis of phraseological units. In turn, phraseology enriches all of the above disciplines, thanks to the features of the subject of study.

Phraseological units (phraseologisms) fill the gaps in the lexical system of the language, which can not fully provide the name of all sides of reality, and are often the only signs of them. When a phraseology has a lexical synonym, it usually differs in stylistic terms. Thrazeology is the treasure trove of language. In phraseology, the history of the people, the originality of their culture and everyday life is reflected. Thrazeologisms are often brightly national in nature. Along with purely national phraseologisms, English phraseology also has many international phraseologisms. The English phraseological fund is a complex conglomerate of native and borrowed phraseologisms with obvious prevalence of the former.

Thrazeologisms are highly informative units of language, they cannot be considered as "ornaments" or "excesses". Thrazeologisms are one of the language universals, as there are no languages without phraseology. English phraseology is very rich and has a long history.

Thrazeologisms - semantically related groups of words that are formed outside the general rules of word selection and combination. The term "phraseological unit" denotes several semantically different types of expressions: *idioms* are characterized by lack of motivation and have an integral nominal function; *proverbs and sayings are formed* in folklore and *winged words* - aphoristic expressions, usually belonging to a specific author or some anonymous literary source.

It should be noted that the views of different authors on the term "phraseological unit" do not coincide. For example, I.V. Arnold prefers the term "stable expressions" as a consequence of the uncertainty of the terms "phraseology" and "idiom" adopted in the linguistics of our country. There are many opinions on the definition, classification, description and analysis of this part of the vocabulary. Moreover, there are no two researchers whose views on the terminology used are the same. The word "phraseology", for example, has different meanings in our country, in the UK and the USA.

In Russian linguistic literature, this term is used for a whole group of expressions where the meaning of one element depends on the other, regardless of the structure and properties of the expression (V.V. Vinogradov); according to other authors, it defines only such stable expressions that, unlike idioms, do not have expressiveness or emotional coloring (A.I. Smirnitsky). N.N. Amosova overcomes the subjectivity of the above definitions by insisting on applying this term only to expressions that she calls "unity with a stable context," i.e. unity where it is impossible to replace any of the components "without changing the meaning of not only the entire expression, but also those of its elements that have remained unchanged. A.V. Kunin singles out the structural peculiarity of the elements of phraseological unity, the change in the value of the whole, as opposed to its elements taken separately, and determines the degree of stability.

In English and American linguistics the meaning of the term "phraseology" differs significantly from the meaning adopted in the national linguistics. The concept of "phraseology" is stylistic, meaning "mode of expression, word choice, style" (New Webster's Dictionary of the English Language / Delhi, 1989).

The word "idiom" is even more polysemantic. The English use it to define a method of expression peculiar to the language, without distinguishing between grammatical and lexical levels. It can also mean a group of words whose meaning is difficult or impossible to understand, knowing the meaning of individual words. Moreover, "idiom" can mean a synonymous word "language" or "dialect," indicating a form of expression peculiar to a nation, country, region, or one person.

The term "stable expression", on the contrary, is more defined and understandable as the first element highlights the most important characteristic of these units, namely, their stability and certainty.

Some linguists attribute phraseology to the vocabulary of a language, but phraseology is part of lexicology, mainly because phraseological units are considered equivalent to words and lexicology as a discipline that studies words and their equivalents. This is why the theory of the equivalence of phraseology to words deserves more detailed consideration. Charles Bally noted that a common feature of all phraseological units is the possibility or impossibility to replace it with a single word, which he called "word identifier" (Bally 1905).

This point of view is quite controversial. The semantic integration of a phraseological unit cannot be defined in this way, since some expressions may have words-synonyms. For example: ***to look fixedly*** - *to stare,* etc. In addition, many phraseological units do not have word identifiers and can only be defined with a different word combination, for example: ***drink like a fish*** - *drink too much,* etc. It should also be noted that proverbs and sayings, i.e. phraseological units with sentence structure, can be defined only with the help of a sentence, e.g.: words of ***feather flock together*** - *people who have the same interest, ideas etc are attracted to each other and stay close together.*

The term "word-equivalent" belongs to L.V. Shcherba. He noted that such word combinations denote one concept and are a potential word-equivalent (Scherba 1915).

The relations between verbal phraseological units and their lexical synonyms - words-identifiers - were studied in the paper, which revealed significant differences between them (Rudenko 1981). It is known that phraseological units and their lexical synonyms express the same meaning in different ways, i.e., they have different types of nomination. Words are used in their literary meaning, which is typical for the primary type of nomination, and phraseological units belong to the secondary type of nomination.

Outstanding linguists, academicians F.F. Fortunatov, A.A. Chess and others have prepared the ground for the syntactic analysis of stable expressions. Many Russian linguists expressed great interest in the theoretical aspects of the problem both in general and in its individual parts. A special branch of linguistics - phraseology - has appeared in our country. V.V. developed the most outstanding theories. V. Vinogradov and B. A. Larin. As for the English language, the number of works on its phraseology is even impossible to calculate. Suffice it to say that there is an English-Russian dictionary of phraseology by A.V. Kunin, supplemented by articles by N.N. Amosova and A.V. Kunin.

B.A. Larina diachronichen approach. His classification reflects three successive stages that pass through stable expressions in the development process. In the first stage, it is simply a free word combination. At the second stage, it is already a motivated stereotypical metaphorical expression. In the third stage, it is an idiom with lost motivation. The meaning of an expression becomes clear to the listener not as a set of values of its elements, but as the meaning of the whole expression.

Classification of Academician V.V. Vinohradov is synchronous. His articles on

Russian phraseology had a huge impact on linguists both in our country and abroad. His classification is based on the motivation of phraseological units, or on the relationship between expression and meaning of its components. The degree of motivation correlates with the stability, indivisibility, and semantic coordination of an expression, i.e., with the possibility of the form or order of its components and the replacement of the entire expression by a single word. According to motivation and other attributes, the phraseological units are divided into three types: phraseological bonds, phraseological unity and phraseological combinations. **Phraseological joints**, or **idioms,** as the name suggests, represent the highest degree of fusion. The meaning of the components is fully absorbed by the meaning of the entire expression, its expressiveness and emotional properties. For example: ***red tape*** - *bureaucracy,* ***to chew the rag*** - *to chatter*. The phraseological fusions are specific in each language and do not lend themselves to literary translation into other languages.

Phaseological unity is more numerous. They are clearly motivated. Emotional quality is based on a metaphorical image created by the expression as a whole. For example: ***to wash one's dirty linen in public, to show one's teeth***. Another characteristic of expressions of this type is the possibility of synonymous substitution without changing the meaning of the whole expression, which, however, can be very limited. Some of these expressions can be easily translated and are even international: ***to know the way the wind blows*** - ***to know*** *where* ***the wind blows.***

The third group in this classification is phraseological combinations that are not only motivated, but also contain a component used in its direct meaning, while the other is used metaphorically: ***to meet the requirements***. The mobility of expressions of this type is much higher than that of previous types. For phraseological combinations, substitutions can be chosen that do not destroy the meaning of the metaphorical element: ***to meet the necessity, the demand***. Such substitutions are not synonymous, and the meaning of the whole expression changes, while the meaning of the verb remains unchanged.

The weakness of this classification was noted by several researchers. When trying to apply it to the English language, you should be aware of certain limitations.

V.V. Vinogradov included in his classification proverbs, two-member technical terms and stereotypical combinations that do not show contextual changes in meaning. And finally, this classification does not get a general theoretical basis, and being developed for the Russian phraseology, it does not reflect the specific features of the English language.

Professor A.I. Smirnitsky considers a phraseological unit to be similar to a single word in that the relationship between its parts is idiomatic, so that it has a significant semantic integrity and is included in speech as one unit. He considers the difference between a lexical unit (word) and a phraseological unit to be structural and uses the term "separateness" to describe the lack of structural integrity. He distinguishes three classes of word combinations: **traditional word combinations**, which, repeated many times in speech, are not represented by word equivalents. The value of traditional word combinations is derived from the sum of their component values, for example: *clenched fists - compressed fists, rough sketch - rough sketch, sketch; to shrug one's shoulders - shrug*. Idiomatics is the main characteristic of **phraseological units**, which distinguishes them from the combination of words during speech. Phraseological units are constantly used in English speech and are part of the basic tissue of the language, are its integral part. They are devoid of figurativeness and metaphoricality. If there is an image that underlies a phraseological unit, then only in terms of origin. Examples of expressions of this class are: *to get up - to get up (wake up), to fall in love - to fall in love, to be surprised - to be surprised,* etc. **Idioms** are based on the transfer of meaning, a metaphor clearly understood by the speakers. They are characterized by a bright stylistic coloring, emotional saturation, a departure from neutral style. For example: *to take the bull by the horns - to take the bull by the horns; to wash one's dirty linen in public - to take the dirt out of the hut; to fish in troubled waters - to catch fish in muddy waters.*

Only the second class of word combinations - phraseological units - was analyzed and classified in detail; further more detailed classification is rather haphazard and contains structural, stylistic and semantic criteria. This classification had a much smaller impact than V.V.'s classification. Vinogradov, however, in its approach to stable word combinations, it can be very useful, since the most important features of the English language are noted here.

We find a different understanding of phraseological units in the works of N.N. Amosova. She singles out two types of phraseological units, namely, fragments and idioms (Amosova 1963). **Phrases** are units of constant context, where the index minimum required to actualize a given value of a semantically realizable word is the only possible constant, e.g.: ***beef tea, to knit one's brows, black frost***. The second component is an index minimum for the first one. It should be noted that single compatibility in many phrases is extremely unstable and they easily pass into combination variables of words. N.N. Amosova herself also admits that phrases are the most fluid part of the phraseological fund (Amosova 1964). **Idioms,** as opposed to phrases, are units of constant context where the index minimum and the semantically realizable element normally form an identity and both are represented by the common lexical composition of the word combination. Idioms are characterized by a holistic meaning, e.g. ***red tape - red tape, red tape,*** *bureaucracy;* ***to play with fire*** - *play with fire,* etc. N.N. Amosova also singled out partial-predicative phraseologisms - revolutions, which contain a grammatically leading member - an antecedent, and a predictive unit depending on it, for example: ***see how the land lies*** - *to find out how things are;* ***pass in the night*** - *fleeting meetings,* etc. N.N. Amosov does not include stable rotations with an all-predictive structure in his phraseology. N.N. Amosova based her classification on only one principle, which was a disadvantage or, as S.G. Gavrin notes, a "vulnerable point" of her concept, since she reduces the whole variety of phraseological phenomena to one factor - phraseological compatibility (Gavrin 1974).

A.I. Yefimov has the widest understanding of the volume of phraseology. He attributed to the phraseological means of language idioms, proverbs, aphorisms of writers, winged lines of poems, stable formulas, turns of scientific and technical character (Yefimov 1961).

S.G. Gavrin widely understands the scope of phraseology, which is suitable for the phraseological system in terms of functional and semantic complicability (Gavrin 1974). S.G. Gavrin managed to create a coherent classification of phraseology in modern Russian.

On the example of the phraseological turns of the model "verb + noun" in the Russian language, N.M. Shansky distinguishes three types of semantic relations between a verb and a noun within the limits of phraseology: 1) a verb and a noun are semantically equal, and both are semantic *(beating eggplant, setting a dragonfly, sitting in a puddle,* etc.).); 2) a noun is used as a semantic component of the revolution, while the verb is lexically empty and serves only to express purely grammatical meanings; 3) a verb, a noun or a semantically empty word with a purely expressive character is used as a semantic component of the revolution *(to settle / to settle nonsense, etc.),* or acts as a peculiar morph *(to close / to close eyes).*

The first type of semantic ratio between a verb and a noun is observed in phraseological combinations and phraseological units, the third type is typical for phraseological combinations. As for the second, it is found in such phraseological combinations of different semantic commonalities, which are "periphrases" of simple verbs containing a noun of the same root as the corresponding verb *(cope/reference, look/look, etc.).*

Thus, the exceptional complexity of the object of research - phraseological units - explains the different points of view that linguists adhere to in determining the phraseological units, their classification. Of great importance is the angle from which a scientist approaches the classification of phraseological units. For A.I. Smirnitsky, one of the most important parameters of phraseology is the equivalence of phraseology to word; for N.N. Amosova, the type of constant context; for S.G. Gavrin, functional-semantic complicability. A.I. Smirnitsky and N.N. Amosova have a narrow understanding of the scope of phraseology, while S.G. Gavrin has a broad one.

1.3 Phraseomatics: definition and phraseomatic value

While studying different classifications of phraseological units, special attention should be paid to the classification proposed by A.V. Kunin. The peculiarity of this classification is that A.V. Kunin believes that phraseology consists of three sections: **idiomatics**, **idiophraseomatics**, and **phraseomatics**. This classification includes the one proposed by V.V. Kunin. Vinogradov, clarifies and supplements it. The need for a new classification arose due to the fact that English phraseology does not fit into the three classes of phraseology identified by V. V. Vinogradov.

<u>Idiomatics</u> includes actual phraseological units or idioms, i.e. stable combinations of lexemes with fully or partially reinterpreted meaning.

<u>Idiophraseomatics</u> includes idiophraseomatic units, i.e. stable word combinations, in the first phrase-semantic variants of which the components have literal but complicated meanings, and in the second phrase-semantic variants - completely reconsidered. For example: ***chain reaction*** *1) chain reaction (a scientific term); 2) chain reaction (a completely reinterpreted idiomatic variant).* The second variant - rethinking of the first, which is its prototype. Rethinking is metaphorical.

Phraseomatics includes phraseomatic units of non-idiomatic character, but with a complicated meaning.

Based on this division, linguists select three types of phraseological value: idiomatic value, idiomatic value and phraseological value. These types of value are part of the phraseological microsystem of the language, which makes it possible to determine their varieties according to the structural and semantic features of the phraseological units of each class.

The term "phraseological meaning" was suggested in 1964 independently by two authors (Arkhangelsky 1964, Kunin 1964). Justification of phraseological significance as a linguistic category is complicated by the fact that there are different understandings of a phraseological unit, its component composition and the volume of phraseology.

The notion of a phraseological meaning will be more justified and distinguished from lexical meaning if we also take into account the peculiarities of constructing a phraseological unit: "... it seems necessary to make an attempt to find common differentiating features of different types of linguistic meaning, because otherwise the linguist will constantly face the danger of mixing linguistic phenomena of different order or of actually recognizing a single and homogeneous semantic basis for all structural elements of language" (Zvegintsev 1957).

Phraseological value cannot be realized outside certain structures. In English there are seven main structural types of phraseologisms.

1. Single-core phraseological units, i.e. revolutions consisting of one significant and one service lexeme or one significant and two or three service lexemes *(at large - in general, all; **by the way - by the way; out of the way** - remote)*. By service lexemes we mean lexemes that do not function as independent members of a sentence and serve to connect words in a sentence (prepositions, unions), as well as to characterize a number, certainty or uncertainty of nouns (articles).

2. Phraseological units with the structure of subordinate or compositional word combinations *(**to burn one's fingers - to burn one's fingers - to burn one's fingers; high and mighty** - the powers of this world)*.

3. Phaseological units with partially predictive structure *(lexema + appendage sentence),* **which pass in the night** *- fleeting meetings.*

4. Phraseological units with the structure of the appendage sentence: ***when pigs fly*** *- "when **pigs fly**", never.*

5. Nominative-communicative phraseological units, i.e., verb turns with the structure of the word combination with the verb in the infinitive and with the structure of the sentence with the verb in the passive voice *(**to break the ice - the ice is broken**)*.

6. Phraseological units with a simple or complex sentence structure *(**birds of feather flock together - a fisherman can see any green in my eyes** from afar? **- Do I** seem so gullible to you?, **God damn it!** - damn it!, damn it!, dumb abyss!)*.

7. Equivalents of the sentence, i.e. some structural types of intermodule turns having the power of speech and characterized by an independent intonation *(**by George!** - god sees!, honestly!; **my foot!** - so I believed!; - the hell with two!, the hell with a bald one!)*. Attribution of interjections of this structural type to the equivalents of the sentence is not indisputable, as evidenced by V.V.'s statement. Vinogradov: "The question whether interjections of a sentence form and can form and whether they are "word-proposals" is still the subject of lively debate among syntaxists" (Vinogradov 1947).

The notion "information invariant" is important for determination of phraseological value. I.S. Narsky understands the invariant of invarnation as "something that is stably preserved during transformation of information". (Narsky 1969).

Phraseological value is an invariant of information expressed by semantically complicated, separately formed language units not formed by generating structurally semantic models of variable word combinations (Kunin 1986).

This understanding of the phraseological value makes it possible to determine its three main varieties: idiomatic value, idiophraseomatic value and phraseological value.

Idiomatic value is an invariant of information expressed by separate language units with fully or partially reinterpreted values.

Idio-phrase-semantic value is an invariant of information expressed by separate language units, some of which have literal but complicated meanings and others which are their derivatives, are completely rethought.

Phraseomatic value is an invariant of information expressed by separate language units with unreasonable but complicated meaning.

§ 2 Language, as an object of study of cognitive linguistics

Cognitive Linguistics is a branch of linguistic functionalism that believes that the linguistic form is derived from the functions of language. Special importance is given to cognitive functions and it is assumed that the other functions are derived from them or reduced to them. The focus of cognitive linguistics is language as a universal cognitive mechanism.

Cognitive approach to language - the belief that the language form is ultimately a reflection of cognitive structures, i.e., the structures of human consciousness, thinking, cognition. Among the most important cognitive phenomena that determine the language form are: structures of knowledge representation, natural categorization, long-term memory, RAM, attention, activation.

It is important to note that in line with the informational interpretation of the functionalism paradigm, a variety of cognitive concepts are currently being developed in the West. There is a significant connection between the theoretical solution of the problem "psyche (consciousness, knowledge, cognitions) and the brain" and specific developments in the problems of artificial intelligence. It is obvious that in modern conditions the paradigm of functionalism creates the most adequate general theoretical and methodological prerequisites for the development of comprehensive cognitive research in linguistics.

The sphere of vital interests of cognitive linguistics includes "mental" bases of understanding and production of speech in terms of how language knowledge structures are presented and participate in information processing (Kubryakova 1994).

Unlike other disciplines of the cognitive cycle, cognitive linguistics considers those, and only those cognitive structures and processes that are characteristic of a person as homo loquens. Namely, in the foreground there is a systematic description and explanation of the mechanisms of human language learning and the principles of structuring these mechanisms. The following questions arise (Felix, Kanngiesser, Rickheit 1990):

1. Representation of the mental mechanisms of language learning and the principles of their structuring: is it enough to be limited to a single representation - or should these mechanisms be presented within the framework of different representations? How do these mechanisms interact? What is their internal structure?

2. Production. The main question is: are production and perception based on the same units of the system or do they have different mechanisms? In addition, do the processes that make up the production of speech run in parallel or sequentially over time?

3. Perception in a cognitiveistic way is studied somewhat more actively than the production of speech - this is another manifestation of interpretationism. In this regard, the question is: What is the nature of the procedures that regulate and structure language perception? What knowledge is activated through these procedures? What is the organization of semantic memory? What is the role of this memory in perception and understanding of speech?

In cognitive linguistics it is accepted that mental processes are not only based on representations, but also correspond to certain procedures - "cognitive computing". For the rest of the "cognitive disciplines" (especially for cognitive psychology) the conclusions of cognitive linguistics are valuable to the extent that allow to understand the mechanisms of these very cognitive calculations in general.

Thus, the central task of cognitive linguistics is formulated as a description and explanation of the internal cognitive structure and dynamics of the speaker-listener. The speaker-listener is seen as a system of information processing consisting of a finite number of independent components and correlating linguistic information at different levels. The purpose of cognitive linguistics is to investigate such a system and to establish its most important principles, not just to systematically reflect language phenomena.

Some linguists (e.g., generativists) believe that the language system forms a separate module, outside the general cognitive mechanisms. More often than not, however, language activity is seen as one of the moduses of "cognitions", making up the tip of the iceberg, which is based on cognitive abilities that are not purely linguistic, but provide the prerequisites for the latter. These abilities include: the construction of images and the logical conclusion based on them, the acquisition of new knowledge based on existing information, the drafting and implementation of plans. V.Z. Demjankov formulated the following maximum: "Avoid talking about something bypassing human cognitions" (Demjankov 1994).

Thus, as a science engaged in the study of cognitive linguistics and cognitive aspects of lexical, grammatical phenomena, cognitive science focuses on linguistic knowledge in the human head and interacts with cognitive psychology in the analysis of verbal verbal memory, internal lexicon, generation, perception, understanding of speech, how and in what form the words created by human knowledge structures are put on. The analysis of the way the individual's knowledge base is expressed by various linguistic means in speech and the impact on consciousness and understanding of discourse is of greatest interest. Focusing on the processes of generation and cognition of speech, cognitive science deals with the area in which the process of speech production is inextricably linked to the processes taking place in our memory. In addition, it is necessary to take into account "background knowledge", which, according to O.S. Akhmanova, is "mutual knowledge of realities for speakers and listeners, which is the basis of linguistic communication" (Akhmanova 1977). Observation of the behavior of language units in the process of speech production, and the influence of cognitive and pragmatic factors are the goal of the study of the functional approach, which is regarded as an attempt at a more extensive analysis of linguistic phenomena.

2.1. Theoretical foundations of cognitive description of semantics phraseomatic combinations

The basic category of cognitive semantics is a concept that can act as mental entities of different volume and different functional purpose. Concepts form the information basis of the world picture, playing a primary role in the formation of the individual knowledge fund and information transfer. It is through the concepts of *stereotypes of consciousness that* human thought activity is carried out. This term began to be used in the works of Russian linguists relatively recently, despite the fact that back in 1928 S.A. Askoldov-Alexeev in his article "Concept and Word" used the term *"concept",* defining it as a mental formation that replaces us in the process of thinking an undefined set of subjects of the same kind. S.A. Askoldov-Alexeev emphasizes the heterogeneity of the conceptual thought functions: a concept is not always a substitute for real subjects. It can be a substitute for some aspects of an object or real actions, such as the concept of "justice". Finally, it can be a deputy of various purely thought functions. These are, for example, mathematical concepts. The very concept of Askoldov-Alexeev defines as an instant and elusive glimpse of something in consciousness, as the buds of the most complex inflorescences of thought specifics (Askoldov-Alexeev 1997). Initially, "concept" was perceived as synonymous with the word "concept". In "Thesaurus on theoretical and applied linguistics" by S.E. Nikitina synonyms "concept", "signal" are indicated to the term "concept"; to the designation "concept field" is the word combination "conceptual field" (Nikitina 1987). E.M. Mednikova uses the word "concept" when defining the lexical system, putting the same meaning into it. The vocabulary is not just a number of concepts expressed by corresponding units, like a word it is not just a connection of some sound with some concept. A word is a single whole (Mednikova 1974). Gradually the terms "concept" and "concept" began to differentiate. Nowadays, there is no doubt that the mentioned words are not equal. As Y.S. Stepanov explains, a concept exists in the human mental world not in the form of clear concepts but as a *bundle of* ideas, concepts, knowledge, associations, experiences, which accompanies the word (Stepanov 1998).

Detailed description of the structure and content of the concept is given in the "Brief Dictionary of Cognitive Terms" (Kubryakova 1998). "Concept" is defined as an operative, substantial unit of memory, mental lexicon, conceptual system of language and brain (lingua mentalis), the whole picture of the world reflected in human psyche. It is emphasized that the concept of "concept" corresponds to the idea of those senses, which a person operates in the processes of thinking and which reflect the content of experience and knowledge, the content of the results of all human activities and processes of cognition of the world in the form of some "quanta" of knowledge. The concept is interpreted as some basic cognitive essence, allowing to connect the meaning with the used word (Richard 1998), as a substantial unit of the conceptualization process, by means of which reality refracts in the human head.

L.M. Zainullina gives a detailed and thorough description of the concept structure. The author offers a consolidated typology of concepts based on the classifications of J. Lakoff, J. Taylor, E.S. Kubryakova, A.P. Babushkin, Z.D. Popova, I.A. Sternin, N.N. Boldyreva and includes concepts and concepts that are objectified mainly by lexical units of specific semantics (white, round, sparrow, cripples, raccoon): a concept-concept represented by a generalized spatial-graphic or contour scheme; a concept-concept consisting of the most general characteristics of an object or phenomenon, the result of its rational reflection and comprehension; a frame - a multi-component concept conceivable as a whole in its components, a volumetric representation, a certain set of standard knowledge about an object or phenomenon (shopping, hospital, restaurant); scenario (script) - a sequence of several episodes in time and space as a sequence of individual episodes, stages, elements (game, tour, church attendance); propositional structures (propositions) in which the basic predicate and arguments (agent, patient, beneficiary, instrument, etc.) are selected.д.). As indicated in the paper, concepts are divided into stable and unstable, verbalized and hidden, single-level, multi-level and segmental (Zainullina 2003).

The concept determines the semantic potential of a language unit before its implementation in speech, getting a concise or detailed representation in different lexemes. Concept has a logically organized dynamic structure consisting of a source, base element and related elements through the prototypical value of derivative elements (Ryabtseva 1991). The term "concept" includes a three-dimensional, multilevel content that "conveys knowledge of what is meant in all its relationships and relationships. The concept is preceded ontologically by categorization, which creates a typical image and forms a "prototype" (Telia 1996). Apparently, it can be reconstructed on the basis of lexicographical data.

The concept of "concept" refers to the "quanta" of knowledge, which a person operates in the process of thinking, and includes information about the concept in all its relationships. Concepts reduce a variety of observed and imagined phenomena to something common, bringing them under one rubric; they allow to store knowledge about the world and turn out to be building elements of the conceptual system, promoting processing of subjective experience by bringing it under general categories (Kubryakova 1998).

The multiplicity of concepts at different levels, in which the diversity and heterogeneity of knowledge about real life is manifested, has now become evident. Taking into account that concepts have inadequate functional potential, it is reasonable to distinguish different types of mental entities - concepts (i.e. microconcepts), macroconcepts, and superconcepts - when interpreting linguistic material. Concepts oriented to the lexical meaning of an individual lexeme have a small semantic scope and perform an identifying function. They serve for description (portrait) of atomic lexemes. Concepts can also be used for interpretation of lexeme blocks and word classes of rather large volume. In such cases, the language implements macroconcepts that manifest themselves as a semantic category with the highest degree of abstraction and include private concreteness values of general semantics. Macroconcepts are large-scale entities that have a huge systematizing "power". They are surrounded by an extensive semantic domain, which requires a sufficiently large dictionary to describe (Karasik 1999). Macroconcepts like "to live", "to speak", "to move", "to work", "to see", "to hear" are used to identify and systematize large, hierarchically organized lexical categories that can be interpreted as functional-cognitive spheres that act as objects of description in the functional-cognitive dictionary (Kildibekova, Gafarova 1998, 2000, 2001, 2002, 2003). The macroconcept can be subject to numerous semantic refinements and multi-spectrum concretization. Conceptual transformations and deployments of the initial concept are fixed in lexemes of different sizes, which predetermine the multistage structure of the functional-cognitive sphere, and are visually represented in the functional-cognitive dictionary.

Термин «суперконцепт» ориентирован на функциональноThe communicative potential of a global mental unit is manifested in a volumetric macroframe, which consists of a variety of typical syntactic constructions expressing different types of situations related to the basic concept.

The source and starting point for all functional and semantic transformations is the basic concept. Basic concepts are essential concepts that must necessarily be expressed in order for language to be a satisfactory means of communication (Sepir 1993). All elements of the functional-associative potential of the Basis Concept are verbalized in nominal units that organize an entire thesaurus of the corresponding semantic space. The generative function of the basic concept can be compared with the dominant role in the development of the lexico-semantic paradigm. The wider the information potential of the dominant, the greater the possibilities it has. The whole set of verbalized concepts creates the conceptosphere of language, which appears to be a very complex system formed by intersections and interlacing of numerous and diverse structures organizing concepts into rows, chains, fields with the center and periphery, and branching trees with cross-references (Popova 1996).

In a conceptual picture of the world concepts take a special place, being fundamental for human cognition and communication entities. Z.D. Popova and I.A. Sternin rightly emphasize that a concept is a thinking complex unit, which in the process of thinking activity is turned by different sides, actualizing its different features and layers (Popova, Sternin 2002).

The conceptosphere of the national language is the richer the whole culture of the nation is (Likhachev 1997). However, the national-cultural originality of the Conceptual Sphere is invisible from the inside; it can be revealed only in the process of comparative analysis.

According to N.A. Krasavsky, any conceptosphere is objectified by different language techniques - direct, secondary and indirect types of nominations. The most informative in the linguocognitive analysis of the conceptual sphere are the word (lexemic) and super word (free word combinations, phraseologisms) categories, because they serve as a way to generate, develop, receive and store knowledge. The current state and prospects of further development of phraseology are connected with cognitive and linguistic-cultural directions in linguistics. Within the framework of these directions, phraseologies are considered as signs of a special nature associated with the cognitive abilities of a person in general and an individual in particular, and with the communicative intentions of native speakers (Krasavsky 2001). Of particular importance is the consideration of the functional capabilities of phraseomatic units as signs of a secondary motivated nomination, which also carry information about the special, national way of seeing the world by this or that linguocultural community.

Chapter II Conceptual organisation of meanings of English verb name phraseomatic word combinations in the English-language explanatory dictionary

§ 1 Research methodology for functional-cognitive potential of English verb-name phraseological phrases

Целью данной работы является изучение и описание функционально-cognitive potential of English verb-name phraseomatic word combinations, the corpus of which is composed by a continuous vocabulary sample from Longman Dictionary of Contemporary English. To achieve this goal, we use a comparative analysis of the conceptual structures of the English phraseomatic combinations on three lines of characterization of their actions. This provides a full understanding of their functional and cognitive potential.

The method of reconstruction of concept-correlates is based on onomasiological interpretation of definitions of phraseomatic combinations, according to which verb units identify the concept, and other words and labels identify the features of this concept. The main principles of onomasiological interpretation of lexical and phraseological units were developed and stated by V.M. Kalimullina (Kalimullina 1985).

The onomasiological aspect of verb units can be represented as a compound of three types of characterization of the action defined as the onomasiological base of the verb: reference, relative and descriptive characterization (Calimullina 1982). The reference characterization of an action means a reflection of the reference characterization of a verb, i.e., an indication of a specific action. Relative characterization of the action is understood as a reflection of the spatial and temporal characteristics of the action. Descriptive characterization refers to the reflection of the action itself (method, instrument, etc.). It can be considered that the cumulative characterization of an action itself is the result of refraction of a categorical verb "action/process" in three aspects: reference, relative, and descriptive, all aspects of characterization of an action, and are formalized in the onomasiological basis of a verb unit. Each aspect of characterizing the action of a coreferential unit is analyzed on the basis of two parameters: qualitative and quantitative.

A qualitative analysis of the reference characterization indicates the area of verb reference. Identifier verbs were distributed in the following areas of reference: 1) emotional impact *(to impress, to please); 2)* emotional and intellectual attitude *(to respect, to abhor, to doubt);* 3) emotional behavior and expression of feelings (to *fuss, to exclaim)* 4) mental activity (to *think, to conclude);* 5) social contact (to *thank, to demand);* 6) physical purposeful actions *(to rub, to squeeze};* 7) change of physical state (to *change, to improve);* 8) movement (to *move, to step};* 9) sight / sight (to *look, to glance, to peep);* 10) existence, *to exist, to blossom.*

A quantitative analysis of the reference characterization of verbs-indicators shows that they can have a simple reference characterization (one action is called), e.g.: to jeopardize - to endanger; and a complex reference characterization reflecting either two actions related to relations of conjunctiva (*to look - to give attention in seeing)* or two actions related to relations of disjunctiva (to *help - to help or to support).*

Глаголы-идентификаторы могут отражать в относительной характеризации следующие признаки: статичность :: динамичность, отношение к субъекту /объекту действия, предельность :: непредельность, повторяемость :: неповторяемость, продолжительность во   time, place of action.

Accordingly, the identity verbs make up the following oppositions: static :: dynamic *(to live, to be :: to grip, to surrender);* subjective :: субъектнообjective (to *breathe, to decline :: to use, to stress);* limit :: unsaturated (to *glance, to notice :: to exist, to work);* *verbs* that can call action repetition :: verbs that cannot call action repetition *(to glance, to smile):to despair, to starve); verbs that* reflect duration in time :: verbs that do not reflect duration in time *(to gaze, to suspend : to sleep, to ease)*; verbs that indicate the place of action :: verbs that do not indicate the place of action (to *witness :: hope, to observe).*

Identifier verbs are classified into two groups according to the presence/absence of descriptive characterization in their base: verbs without descriptive characterization *(to resemble - to look or be alike; to quarrel - to have an argument)* and verbs with descriptive characterization *(to flee - to escape (from) <u>by hurting away</u>* - method; *to fuss - to act or behave in a nervous, restless and anxious way over small matters* - method + object attribution + evaluation).

The following features of descriptive characterization of action may be reflected in the verb-identifier basis: causation *(to age - <u>to (cause)</u> to become old);* способ *(to glance - to give a <u>rapid</u> look);* инструмент действия *(to laugh - to express amusement, happiness, careless disrespect, etc. by making explosive sounds <u>with the voice,</u> usu. while smiling);* интенсивность *(to drink - to use alcohol, esp. <u>too much);</u>* оценка *(to mistake - to have a <u>wrong</u> idea about);* субъектная отнесенность *(to die - (<u>of creatures and plants)</u> to stop living...);* объектная отнесенность *(to pride on / upon - to be pleased and satisfied with (<u>oneself)</u> about (sth);* ситуативная отнесенность *(to start - to make a quick uncontrolled movement, <u>as from sudden surprise)</u>* и др.

§ 2 The functional and cognitive potential of English verbal-noun phrases

This paragraph describes the functional and cognitive potential of English verb-name phraseology. The body of phraseomatic word combinations was more than 2000 units.

Since this study deals with verb units, we note that it is necessary to take into account the nature of onomasiological refraction of onomasiological verb "action/process" in each case in order to establish the conceptual characteristics of the verb.

In verb names, a multidimensional characteristic of the situation unfolds: in addition to the reflection of the action and the relation of the action to the objects of reality, it is possible to note the development of the action in time, indicate the method, place, and instrument of action. In other words, a characterization of an action can be divided into three types of conceptual features: reference, relative, and descriptive. The reference conceptual feature is understood to be the reference relation of the verb, i.e. an indication of a concrete action. Relative conceptual sign is understood as a space-time characteristic of the action. The descriptive conceptual sign is understood to be the actual sign of action (method, instrument, etc.) (Kalimullina 1996).

We can assume that the cumulative characterization of the action itself is the result of refraction of the categorical onomasiological sign of the verb "action" in three aspects of characterization: the reference, the relative, and the descriptive. The cumulative characterization of the action can be called the conceptual structure of the verb.

Since the conceptual structure of a verb is a set of reference, relative and descriptive conceptual признаков именуемого действия, она отражает его функциональнocognitive potentials.

To study the conceptual structure of phraseomatic combinations of the studied type, one of the most important factors that determine the stability at the level of combination semantics: complicability.

When correlating the conceptual structures of phraseomatic combinations, it turns out that:

The complicability of the grammatical plan reflects the following layouts relative conceptual traits:

dynamism :: static	*to fly into a fury*(quickly become very angry) *:: to glow with pride* (to look very happy because you feel proud etc)
place	*to throw sb into prison* (to suddenly put someone in prison) *to take sb's order* (write down what a customer in a restaurant wants)
single action	*to satisfy a request* (to provide what someone has asked for, what they need etc); *to break the habit* (to stop doing sth that is annoying or bad for your health)
отношение к subject/object actions	*to screw up your courage* (to try to be brave enough to do sth you are very nervous about)/ *to pay attention to* (to give your attention to sth)
attitude towards the person you are talking to or the object of action	*to sing sb's praises* (to praise someone very much) /*to pay tribute to* (to say how much you admire or respect someone or sth)
repeatability :: non-repeatability	*to play a part* (to perform the actions, words etc for a particular character in a play, film etc) *:: to miss the point* (not understand the main meaning of sth)
limit :: the limit	*to realize your potential* (to succeed in doing as well as you possibly can) *:: to show preference to* (to treat someone more favourably than you treat other people)
duration / time	*to pass the time* (when you are bored or

	waiting for sth.) *to press sb's hand/arm (to hold someone's hand or arm tightly for a short time, to show friendship, sympathy etc)*
subject-object focus	*to give sb a peck (to kiss someone quickly and lightly) / to take possession of sth (if you take possession of a house, car, or valuable object, you get it after it has become yours)*
action phase (initial phase)	*to set sail (to begin a journey by boat or a ship)* *to take up a post (start doing an important job)*
action phase (continued)	*to protest your innocence (keep saying that you are innocent)* *to keep your mind on (to keep paying attention to sth even if it is boring or if you want to think about sth else)*
action phase (final phase)	*to starve to death (to die from lack of food); to settle your nerves (to stop your nerves from being upset)*

the complicability of the semantic plan reflects the layering of such

descriptive conceptual traits, such as:

intensity	*to relieve monotony (to make sth less dull and boring)* *to pay tribute to (to say how much you admire or respect someone or sth)*
causation	*to bring sth to life (to make sth live); to set light to (to make sth start burning)*
quantitative description	*to draw a parallel between (to show that two things are similar)* *to hold your drink (if someone can hold their drink, they're able to drink a lot of alcohol without becoming drunk)*
purpose	*to try sb's patience (to make someone lose their patience)* *to gain advantage (to get or try to get sth that will help you against your opponents)*
mode of action	*to fly into a rage (suddenly become very angry);* *to quicken your pace (to walk faster)*

rating	*to lose its shape* (to become the wrong shape) *to commit an offence* (do sth that is an offence)
action forwarding	*to shift the responsibility* (to make someone else responsible for sth, esp. for sth bad that is happened)
situational attribution	*to propose a toast to sb* (to formally ask a group of people at a social event to join you in wishing someone success, happiness etc, while raising a glass of wine and then drinking from it); *to jump a queue* (to go unfairly to the front of a queue instead of waiting)
comparison	*to place a premium on* (to consider one quality as being much more important then others) *to make a reduction* (sell sth more cheaply)
stylistic references	*to present your apologies/compliments etc* ((formal) used to greet someone, apologize to them etc very politely); *to pronounce sentence* ((law) if a judge pronounces sentence he or she tells the court what kind of punishment a criminal will have)
subject-object attribute of action	*to take sb's temperature* (to measure their temperature); *to present your apologies/compliments etc* (used to greet someone, apologize to them etc very politely)
target	*to set standards* (to officially establish rules, standards etc for doing sth); *to make provision for* (to make plans for future needs)

Complexity of mixed character reflects the combination of

layering by attributes of relative and descriptive characterization

actions, for example:

action phase + subject-object orientation + method	*to pick a quarrel (with sb)* (to deliberately start a quarrel)
repeatability + direction + place + stylistic references	*to resume your seat* ((formal) to go back to the seat where you were before)
direction + place + stylistic	*to skim stones* ((BrE) to throw smooth,

attribution + method	*flat stones into a lake, river etc in a way that make them jump across the surface)*
направление + stylistic attribution + method	*to wend your way ((esp. lit.) to move or travel slowly from one place to another)*
attitude to the object of action + target + intensity + method + evaluation	*to take advantage of sb (to treat someone unfairly to get what you want, especially someone who is generous or easily persuaded)*

Volume of complication on the relative aspect of action characterization,

noted in the complicability of combinations, can be calculated in 1-4 features, but they rarely give a combination of all 4 features. Typical are combinations of 1-3 features:

1 attribute	place of action	*to clear your throat (to make a noise in your throat, esp. before you speak, or in order to get someone's attention)*
2 features	направление actions+ dynamism	*to make way (to move to one side so that someone or sth can pass)*
3 features	repeatability + direction + place	*to resume your seat ((formal) to go back to the seat where you were before)*

The volume of a complication on the line of descriptive characterization can

are calculated in 1-4 attributes:

1 attribute	stylistic references	*to prefer charges ((law) to make an official statement that someone has done sth illegal)*
2 features	causation + situational reference	*to give sth prominence (to put sth in a position where it is easily noticed because you think it is important)*
3 features	object attribute + method + target	*to press sb's hand (to hold someone's hand tightly for a short time, to show friendship, sympathy etc)*
4 features	stylistic attribution + method + intensity + subject-object	*to present your apologies ((formal) used to greet someone, apologize to*
	reference	*them etc very politely)*

Volume of complication in relative and descriptive aspects of action characterization,

reflected in the complicability of the combination

mixed character, can be calculated in 2-4 features:

2 features	object attribute + intensity	*to sing sb'spraise(s)* *(to praise someone very much)*
3 features	action phase + stylistic attribution + situational attribution	*to lose the toss* *((esp. BrE) to lose the right to make a choice at the beginning of a game or race, according to the result of tossing a coin)*
4 features	attitude to the object + target + intensity + method	*to take advantage of smb* (to *treat someone unfairly to get what you want, esp. someone who is generous or easily persuaded)*

Analysis of the volume of complication in the semantics of combinations allowed to establish the degree of complicity of combinations, it may be:

<u>High</u>: compliancy has a volume of 3 or more complicating components: ***to pronounce sentence*** *((law) if a judge pronounces sentence he or she tells the court what kind of punishment a criminal will have* (stylistic attribution + object attribution + situational attribution);

<u>low</u>: compliancy has a volume of 1-2 complicating components: ***to feel sb's pulse*** *(to count how many times someone's heart beats in a minute, usu. by feeling their wrist* (situational attribution + method);

<u>zero</u>: the combination has no compliancy: ***to make a purchase*** *(to buy sth).*

The second factor to study the specificity of the conceptual structure of phraseomatic combinations is the distribution of roles between words-components in its formation.

This can be done using the method of phraseomatic application: comparison of definitions of phraseomatic combinations with definitions of direct values of its components, in combination with onomasiological interpretation of their semantics, allows to determine which of the components of phraseomatic combinations plays a leading role in the formation of its nominal potential, including reference, relative and descriptive characteristics.

As a result of such analysis, phraseomatic combinations were divided into three groups depending on the role of components in forming their nominal potential. The reference characterization here is represented by a noun. In these combinations, the nouns used are verbal. Relative characterization is represented by a verb component, since it is the grammatical nucleus of the combination. Descriptive characterization is usually represented by a noun, since it is the semantic nucleus of the combination.

For example:

Phaseomatic combinations and their definitions	The verb and its definition	Noun and its definition	Role of components in characterization		
			referent	Relative	descriptive
make allowances (to let someone behave in a way you would not normally approve of, because you know there are special reasons for their behaviour)	*make - to do sth*	*allowance - the way of behaviour which is not approved of, but there are special reasons for it*	*N*	*V*	*N*
add variety (to make sth more interesting)	*add - to increase the amount of sth by putting sth more with it*	*variety - the differences within a group, set of actions etc that make it interesting*	*N*	*V*	*N*
take advantage (to use a particular situation to do or get what you want)	*take - to accept sth*	*advantage - a particular situation in which you can do or get what you want*	*N*	*V*	*N*

This group includes 27% of phraseomatic word combinations, presented at the LDCE.

The second group includes phraseomatic combinations, where the leading role in the reference characterization belongs to the verb component.

Relative characterization is usually represented by the verb component, while descriptive characterization can be represented by both a noun and a verb:

Phaseomatic combinations and their definitions	The verb and its definition	Noun and its definition	Role of components in characterization		
			referent	Relative	descriptive
swear sb to secresy *(to make someone promise not to tell anyone what you have told them)*	**swear -** *to make someone promise*	**secrecy -** *the process of keeping sth secret, or the state of being kept a secrecy*	*V*	*V*	*N*
fulfil a prediction *(to happen in a way someone has said sth would happen)*	*to happen*	**prediction -** *sth that you say is going to happen*	*V*	*V*	*N*
lose your mind *(to become crazy or mentally ill)*	**lose -** *to become*	**mind -** *crazy/mentally ill*	*V*	*V*	*N*
to save sb's life *(to someone from . dying)*	**save -** *to save sb's life (to prevent someone from dying)*	**life -** *alive, not dead*	*V*	*V*	*V*

The verb component can be used to form all three types of characteristics: reference, relative and descriptive. This group accounted for 54% of the total number of combinations represented in LDCE.

The third group is represented by phraseomatic combinations, where both components play approximately equal role in reference characterization. Relative characterization in phraseomatic word combinations of this group is usually represented by a verb, while descriptive characterization can be represented by both components:

Phaseomatic combinations and their definitions	The verb and its definition	Noun and its definition	Role of components in characterization		
			referent	Relative	descriptive
switch allegiance (to start to support a different person, group etc.)	*switch - to change from one thing to . another,* *unexpectedly*	*allegiance - loyalty to a leader; country, belief etc*	*V+N*	*V*	*V*
lower your voice (to make it quieter)	*lower - to reduce sth in amount, degree, strength etc or to become less*	*voice - the sound that you make when you speak*	*V+N*	*V*	*V*
fly into a fury (quickly become very angry)	*fly into - to suddenly become*	*fury - a feeling of extreme anger*	*V+N*	*V*	*N*
launch an appeal (to make a serious public request for sth)	*launch - to start sth, esp. an official, public or military activity that has was planned*	*appeal - an urgent request for sth important such as money or help, esp. to help someone in a bad situation*	*V+N*	*V*	*N*

This group accounted for 19% of the total number of verb-names.

phraseomatic word combinations presented at LDCE.

As a result, we can say that verb-name phraseomatic combinations are heterogeneous. From the point of view of structure, both components of combinations presented in an explanatory monolingual dictionary play approximately equal roles in forming the nominal potential of these units.

The method of reconstruction of concept-correlates is based on onomasiological interpretation of definitions of phraseomatic combinations, according to which verb units identify the concept, and other words and labels identify the features of this concept.

The analysis of functional-cognitive potentials of phraseomatic combinations showed that they can reflect the action or state along the reference line of characterization. For example: ***to make an apology** (action), **to answer a description** (state)*. The reference line may be simple or complex. Simple reference characterization reflects one action or

state: ***to pitch a camp*** *(to set up a camp for a short time)* - one action (D); ***to bring up the***
rear *(to be at the back of the line of people or in a race)* - one state (C). Complex reference
characterization reflects two or more actions in the relationship of conjunctiion /
disjunction. For example: ***to make an appointment - to*** *arrange or decide a time or place*
for something to happen (D::E); ***to practice a religion*** *- to take part in the ceremonies*
and obey the rules of a religion (D + + D); ***to wield power*** *- to have a lot of power and*
be ready to use it (C + + C).

Концепты-корреляты   phraseomatic combinations allowed
distribute them into different areas of the conceptual sphere:

Эмоциональное поведение: ***to take pity on*** *(to feel sorry for someone and do something*
to help them); ***to swell with pride*** *(to feel very proud);* ***to fly into a fury*** *(quickly become*
very angry);

Умственная деятельность: ***to abandon hope*** *(to decide that you no longer believe in a*
particular idea); ***to draw a moral*** *(to understand what a story or event is teaching you);*
to give sth a miss *(to decide not to do something);*

Речевая деятельность: ***to take leave of somebody*** *(to say goodbye to somebody);* ***to stick***
to the facts *(to talk only about what you are supposed to be talking about or what is*
certain); ***to air your grievances*** *(to tell other people about things that you think are*
unfair);

Физическая деятельность: ***to stiffle a yawn*** *(to try to stop yawning);* ***to slake your thirst***
(to drink so that you are not thirsty any more); ***to relax your hold*** *(to hold something less*
tightly);

Социальный контакт: ***to satisfy a request*** *(to provide what someone has asked for, what*
they need etc); ***to give a thrashing*** *(to beat someone or be beaten violently as a*
punishment); ***to come to the rescue*** *(to help someone in danger or difficulty);*

Изменение состояния: ***to ring the changes*** *(to make changes to sth, not because it needs*
changing but just in order to make it more interesting, more attractive); ***to lose its shape***
(become the wrong shape); ***to come to/gain prominence*** *(to become important and well-*
known);

Виды существования и жизнедеятельности: ***to starve to death*** *(to die from lack of*
food); ***to regain consciousness*** *(wake up after being unconscious);* ***to pass urine /stools/***

blood (to send out sth as a waste material or in waste material from your bladder or bowels);

Целенаправленные <u>физические действия</u>: *to spin a web (to make a web); **to answer the door** (to open the door to see who is there); **to put sth/sb out of action** (if something or someone is out of action, they are broken or injured, so that they cannot move or work);*

<u>Движение</u>: ***to gain/lose height** (if an aircraft gains height or loses height, it moves higher in the sky or it drops lower in the sky); **to wend your way** (to move or travel slowly from one place to another); **to beat a retreat** (to walk away quickly);*

<u>Зрение /обозрение:</u> ***to catch sight of** (suddenly see or notice sth); **to lose sight of** (to stop being able to see someone or sth); **to steal a glance** (to look at someone or sth quickly and secretly).*

Some phraseomatic word combinations can be simultaneously referred to two or more areas of the conceptual sphere. For example: to ***give an opinion** (to say what you think) - speech and mental activity; **to give a reason** (to explain) - speech and mental activity; **to sing smb's praise(s)** (to praise someone very much) - social contact, speech activity, emotional behavior.*

Relative characterization is represented by the following features: <u>Staticity/dynamics</u>: ***to answer the description** (to match the description)/ **to pitch a camp** (to set up a camp for a short period of time);*

<u>Предельность</u>/непредельность: ***to pass judgement** (to give your opinion or criticism); **to set a record** (to achieve a new record)/ **to practice a religion** (to take part in ceremonies and obey the rules of a religion); **to run a temperature** (to have a temperature that is higher then normal).*

<u>Фаза действия (начальная/продолжающая/завершающая</u>): ***to take up residence** ((formal) to start to live in a place)/**to hold a course** (to continue to move in a particular direction)/ **to break with tradition** (to stop doing something in the way it has always been done);*

*Место действия: **to put to sea** (to start a journey on the sea); **to serve a summons** (to officially send or give someone a written order to appear in a court of law); **to lead the way** (to walk at the front of a group of people);*

Направление: *to beat a retreat* (to walk away quickly); *to hold a course* (to continue to move in a particular direction); *to wend your way* ((esp. lit) to move or travel slowly from one place to another);

Продолжительность <u>во</u> времени: *to pitch a camp* (to set up a camp for a short period of time); *to work up an appetite* (to make yourself hungry especially by doing physical exercise or waiting a long time before you eat or drink); *to wait your chance (to do sth)* (to wait until you have the best conditions to succeed in doing sth). <u>Субъектно-объектная</u> направленность: *to make sb's acquaintance* ((formal) to meet someone for the first time); *to trample sb to death* (to kill someone by stepping heavily on them); *to throw sb into confusion* (to suddenly make a group of people very confused and uncertain about what they should do);

<u>Повторяемость</u>/неповторяемость: *to renew a friendship* (to start a relationship again); *to restore confidence* (to make a person or a group feel confident again)/*to declare war (on sb)* (to announce publicly and officially that you are going to fight a war); *to raise the alarm* (to warn people about danger).

Descriptive description is presented by the following set of features:

Цель: *to make an appearance* (to be present in a court of law for a trial you are involved in); *to take advantage of something* (to use a particular situation to do or get what you want); *to run drugs* (to bring drugs into a country illegally in order to sell them);

Способ: *to tender your resignation* (officially say that you are going to leave your job); *to wend your way* (to move or travel slowly from one place to another); *to run guns* (to bring guns into a country illegally in order to sell them);

Степень: *to lower your voice* (to make it quieter); *to gain height* (to move higher in the sky); *to relax rules/controls/regulations etc* (to make rules etc less strict);

Оценка: *to act the fool* (to behave in a stupid and annoying way); *to turn somebody's head* (to be attractive in a romantic or sexual way to a particular person); *to lose its shape* (to become the wrong shape);

Каузация: *to admit defeat* (to stop trying to do something because you realize you cannot succeed); *to abandon ship* (to leave a ship because it is sinking); *to smack your lips* (to make a short loud noise with your lips because you are hungry);

<u>Субъектно-объектная</u> отнесенность: *to give somebody a tinkle* (to call someone on the

*telephone); **to wring sth's neck** (to kill sth such as a chicken, by twisting its neck); **to give sb a tickle** (to rub someone lightly with your fingers in order to make them laugh);*

Ситуативная <u>отнесенность:</u> ***to come to the rescue*** *(to help someone in danger or difficulty);* ***to accept somebody's apology*** *(to say that you are no longer angry with someone after they have said they were sorry about something they have done, forgive them, after they have apologized);* ***to steal a kiss*** *(to kiss someone quickly when you are not expecting it).*

Стилистическая отнесенность: ***to shed tears*** *((esp.lit.) to cry);* ***to give something a scrub*** *((esp.BrE) to clean something by rubbing it hard);* ***to sustain defeat*** *((formal) to be defeated or lose a lot of soldiers , money etc).*

Интенсивность: ***to sneak a look at*** *(to look at sth quickly and secretly, especially sth that you are not supposed to see);* ***to reduce sb to tears*** *(to make someone cry, especially by being unkind to them);* ***to throw sb into confusion*** *(to suddenly make a group of people very confused and uncertain about what they should do);*

Намеренность: ***to advance your interests*** *(to do something that will help you achieve advantage of success);* ***to gain advantage*** *(to get or try to get something that will help you against your opponents);* ***to mean mischief*** *(to intend to cause trouble);*

Переадресация действия: ***to swear sb to secrecy/silence*** *(to make someone promise not to tell anyone what you have told them);* ***to accept responsibility*** *(to accept that you were responsible for something bad that happened);* ***to pin the blame on*** *(to blame someone for something, often unfairly).*

Conclusion

Comparative analysis of functional-cognitive potentials of phraseomatic combinations showed that along the reference line of characterization they can reflect the action or state. For example: *to make an apology* (action), to answer a description (state). The reference line may be simple or complex. Simple reference characterization reflects one action or state: to pitch a camp (to set up a camp for a short time) - one action (D); to bring up the rear (to be at the back of a line of people or in a race) - one state (C). A complex reference characterization reflects two or more actions in the conjunctiva/disincentive relationship. For example: to make an appointment - *to* arrange or decide a time or place for something to happen (D::E); to practice a religion - to take part in the ceremonies and obey the rules of a religion (D:++D); to wield power - to have a lot of power and be ready to use it (C:++C).

Концепты-корреляты   phraseomatic combinations allowed distribute them into different areas of the conceptual sphere:

Эмоциональное поведение: to take pity on (to feel sorry for someone and do something to help them); to swell with pride (to feel very proud); to lay the blame (to blame someone for something that has happened);

Умственная деятельность: to abandon hope (to decide that you no longer believe in a particular idea); to venture an opinion (to say what you think); to give sth a miss (to decide not to do something);

Речевая деятельность: to take leave of somebody (to say goodbye to somebody); to stick to the facts (to talk only about what you are supposed to be talking about or what is certain); to air your grievances (to tell other people about things that you think are unfair);

Физическая деятельность: to stiffle a yawn (to try to stop yawning); to slake your thirst (to drink so that you are not thirsty any more); to relax your hold (to hold something less tightly);

Социальный контакт: to satisfy a request (to provide what someone has asked for, what they need etc); to give a thrashing (to beat someone or be beaten violently as a punishment); to come to the rescue (to help someone in danger or difficulty).

Some phraseomatic combinations can be simultaneously assigned to two or more areas of the conceptual sphere.

For example:

to give an opinion (to say what you think) - speech and mental activity; to give a reason (to explain) - speech and mental activity; to sing somebody's praise(s) (to praise someone very much) - social contact, speech activity, emotional behavior.

Relative characterization can be represented by the following features:

Статичность/динамичность: to answer the description (to match the description) / to pitch a camp (to set up a camp for a short period of time)/

Предельность/непредельность: to pass judgement (to give your opinion or criticism) / to practice a religion (to take part in ceremonies and obey the rules of a religion);

Action phase (start/end):

to take up residence ((formal) to start to live in a place) / to break with tradition (to stop doing something in the way it has always been done);

Location: to put to sea (to start a journey on the sea);

Direction: to beat a retreat (to walk away quickly);

Duration in time: to pitch a camp (to set up a camp for a short time).

Descriptive characterization can be represented by the following set of features:

Цель: to make an appearance (to be present in a court of law for a trial you are involved in);

Способ: to render your resignation (officially say that you are going to leave your job);

Степень: to lower your voice (to make it quieter);

Оценка: to turn somebody's head (to be attractive in a romantic or sexual way to particular person);

Причина: to abandon ship (to leave a ship because it is sinking);

Subject-object relation: to give somebody a tinkle (to call someone on the phone);

Situation: to come to the rescue (to help someone in danger or difficulty);

Stylistic references: to shed tears ((esp. literary) to cry).

The analysis shows that the conceptual structure of the English verb-name phraseomatic combinations is quite diverse: all three types of conceptual traits take part in forming the structure of the English verb-name phraseomatic combinations. In the majority of combinations, the reference characterization is represented by one or two actions, which seems to be natural when considering verbological phraseology.

Relative characterization is more often represented by static/dynamic, limit/uncertainty, relationship to the subject/object of action/state, less often this type of characterization is represented by duration in time, place of action, direction of action, action phase.

Descriptive characterization in most expressions is reflected rather poorly, more often it is represented by signs of the mode of action, cause or purpose.

Thus, we can conclude that the reference characterization in the word combinations of this type is presented quite brightly, which cannot be said about relative and descriptive types of characterization. It can speak that for formation of the conceptual organization the reference characterization is the basic, and relative and descriptive are only secondary in formation of sense of phraseomatic combinations.

Literature

1. Alekhina A.I. Phrazeological unit and word: To study the phraseological system. - Minsk: Lenin State University Publishing House, 1979.

2. Amosova N.N. Basics of English Phraseology; LSU Publishing House, 1963-206s.

3. Amosova N.N. Frames as a Variety of English Phraseological Units -M.-L., 1964.p.139.

4. Апресян Ю.Д. Фразеологические синонимы типа «глагол + noun" in modern English: Author's thesis ... Cand. phil. - M.:1956.

5. Arnold I.V. Lexicology of Modern English (in English)-L.M.: Enlightenment, 1966.

6. Arnold I.V. Semantic structure of a word in modern English and the method of its research. - L.: Enlightenment, 1966.

7. Arnold I.V. Equivalence as a linguistic concept. - Foreign Languages at School, 1976. №1.

8. V.L. Arkhangelsky. Stable phrases in modern Russian. - Rostov-on-Don, 1964.

9. Askoldov-Alexeev, S.A. Concept and word (in Russian) // Russian literature: Anthology (in Russian) / Under edition of V.P. Neroznaka. - Moscow: Academia, 1997.

10. Ахманова О.С. Гюббенет И.В. "Vertical context" as in philological problem. Problems of Linguistics, 1977. № 3.

11. A.P. Babushkin Types of concepts in the lexico-phraseological system of the Russian language. - Voronezh: Voronezh Un-ta Publishing House, 1996.

12. A.P. Babushkin. Conceptual Types of Meanings of a Word // Contrastive Studies of Lexicon and Phraseology of the Russian Language: Collected Articles - Voronezh: Voronezh Unta, 1996.

13. Babushkin, A.P. Phrazeological concepts // Cognitive linguistics: Collected articles. - Tambov, 1998.

14. Bally S. French Stylistics. - Moscow: Foreign Publishing House, 1961

15. Batyrova A.F. Functional and cognitive potential of English verb-name phraseomatic combinations / Collection of scientific works "Communicative and

functional language description". Part 2. Ufa, BashSU, 2004.

16. Batyrova A.F. Functional and cognitive potential of English and Russian verb-name phraseomatic word combinations and its deployment in the text. Autoref. disk. ... Cand. phil. Volgograd, 2005.

17. Batyrova A.F. Functional and cognitive significance of English and Russian verb-name phraseological expressions. Ufa, BashSU, 2006.

18. Batyrova G.Z. Functional-semantic significance of English and Russian verb phraseological units. Cand. Ph. Ufa, 1999.

19. Belyaevskaya E.G. On some aspects of stability of phraseomatic combinations. M.Torez, ext.131.-M., 1978. pp.16-34.

20. Bitokova S.H. Component composition of combinations of type to give a look and specificity of their functioning. ACD. - M., 1982.

21. Bitokova S.H. Nominative correlation of stable verb words and single words// Word in language and speech. - Nalchik, 1982. - C.17

22. Boldyrev N.N. Conceptual Space of Cognitive Linguistics. №1 2004 г.

23. V.V. Vinogradov. About basic types of phraseological units in Russian // Academician A.A. Chess (1864-1920): [Collected articles] / Under edition of S.P. Obnorskiy. - M.-L., 1947.

24. Vinogradov V.V. Selected works. Moscow: Nauka, 1977. - 312 c.

25. Gavrin S.G. Phrazeology of Modern Russian Language: /In the aspect of the theory of reflection/.-Perm, 1974.-269s.

26. Gafarova G.V., Kildibekova T.A. Cognitive aspects of language lexical system. - Ufa: BashSU, 1998.

27. Gafarova G.V., Kildibekova T.A. Theoretical bases and principles of functional-cognitive dictionary compiling. - Ufa: BashSU, 2003.

28. R.O. Ginzburg, S.S. Hidekel, G.Yu. Knyazeva, A.A. Sankin The course of lexicology of modern English. Higher School, 1966. - 276c.

29. Dashevskaya V.L. Fraseomatic complexes and compatibility problem. - Coll. of scientific articles by V.L. Dashevskaya. M. Torez Scientific Research Institute, vol. 145, 1979.

30. Dashevskaya V.L. Occasional Conversions of Verbal Phraseomatic Complexes. -

Coll. of Scientific Thr. M. Torez, vol. 168, Moscow: 1980.

31. Демьянков В.З. Cognitive Linguistics as a Variety интерпретирующего подхода // Вопросы языкознания. - 1994, №4 - с. 1733.

32. Demyankov V.Z., Kubryakova E.S. Cognitive linguistics // Brief Dictionary of cognitive terms / Kubryakova E.S., Demyankov V.Z., Pankratz Yu.G., Luzina L.G. - M.: Philological f-t of Lomonosov Moscow State University, 1996. - CCP, p. 53-55.

33. Yefimov A.I. Stylistics of Artistic Speech.-M., 1961.

34. V.P. Zhukov Correlation of a phraseological unit and its components with words of free use. - NDVSh, Philological Sciences, 1962, No. 3.

35. Zhukov V.P. About incommensurability of components of phraseology with the word. - Russian Language at School, 1969, №3.

36. Zhukov V.P. Lexico-semantic system in its relation to the phraseological. - The Questions of Description of the Lexico-Semantic System of Language: Abstracts of Scientific Conf. -M.: 1971.

37. Zhukov, V.P. Semantics of Phrase Turns-M.:Prosv.,1978.

38. Zainullina L.M. Linguocognitive research of objective vocabulary on the material of English, Russian, Bashkir, French and German languages. - RIO BashSU, Ufa: 2003.

39. Zvegintsev V.A. Semaciology. - M., 1957.

40. Kalimullina V.M. Nominative lexico-phraseomatic paradigm in English. - Coll. of scientific articles by V.M. Kalimullin. M. Toreza, vol. 171, Moscow: 1981.

41. Kalimullina V.M. System description of the lexicofraseomatic paradigm. Deposited to the Institute of Information Technologies of the USSR Academy of Sciences. - Bulletin "New Soviet Literature on Social Sciences. Linguistics. - №12, M.: 1981.

42. Kalimullina V.M. Nominative correlation of phraseomatic verb-name word combinations and verb-identifiers. - Cand... cand. phil. of sciences. - M.: 1982.

43. Kalimullina V.M. Multilevel paradigms in verb vocabulary: Textbook. - Ufa, edition of Bashkir University, 1985.- 80 p.

44. Kalimullina V.M. The role of verb lexical and phraseologica units in

implementing language functions in the text. Autoref. dis. of Dr. Phil. Krasnodar, 1996.

45. Kalimullina V.M., Batyrova A.F. Complication as a semantic base for description of onomaseology of phraseomatic word combinations / Collection of scientific papers "Communicative and functional language description". Ufa, BashSU, 2003.

46. Kalimullina V.M., Batyrova A.F. The role of English phraseomatic combinations in the development of the concept-correlate their synonyms / Collection of scientific papers "Communicative and functional description of language". Ufa, BashSU, 2004.

47. Kalimullina V.M., Nuriakhmetova Y.M. Nominative potential of English verb-name phraseomatic combinations / Collection of scientific papers "Communicative and functional description of language". Ufa, BashSU, 2004.

48. Karasik V.I. Religious discourse // Linguistic personality: Problems of linguoculturology and functional semantics. - Volgograd: The change. - 1999.

49. Krasavsky N.A. Emotional concepts in German and Russian linguocultures. - Volgograd, 2001.

50. Kubryakova E.S. Parts of speech in onomasiological illumination. - Moscow: Nauka, 1978.

51. Kubryakova E.S. Initial stages of cognitive formation: linguistics - psychology - cognitive science// Problems of linguistics, 1994.№4.p.34- 47.

52. Kubryakova E.S. Parts of speech from the cognitive point of view. M.: 1997.

53. Kubryakova E.S. Concise dictionary of cognitive terms. M.: 1998.

54. Kunin A.V. English phraseology (Theoretical Course). - Moscow: Higher School, 1970. - 342 c.

55. Kunin, A.V. Double actualization as a concept of phraseological stylistics // In. languages at school.

56. Kunin A.V. About phraseological compatibility. - Collection of Scientific Proceedings of the I.V. Kunin Moscow State Institute of Fine Arts. M. Torez, vol. 145, Moscow: 1979.

57. Kunin A.V. English-Russian phraseological dictionary. Moscow: Russian

Language, 1984.

58. Kunin A.V. Course of phraseology of modern English. -M.: Higher School, 1986. -336s.

59. Krasavsky N.A. Emotional concepts in German and Russian linguccultures. Volgograd, 2001.

60. Likhachev, D.S. Conceptosphere of the Russian Language (in Russian) // Izv. - 1993. - T.52 - №1.

61. Likhachev D.S. Selected Works: in 3 volumes, T.2 L., 1997.

62. Lukavchenko I.M. Types of Related Significance and Stable Word Complexes in Modern English (on the material of word combinations of V+N type): Autoref... .cand.phil. of sciences. M.: 1983

63. Mednikova E.M. Meaning of a word and methods of its description. (On the material of modern English). - Moscow: Higher School, 1974.

64. Mescheriakova M.P. Combinations of the type to make a mistake of с точки зрения их синтаксического использования в предложении // Вопросы РоманоGermanic philology and foreign language teaching methods. - Sverdlovsk, 1967.

65. Mova V.I. Design type to give a laugh in modern English. AKD, - Moscow, 1965.

66. Mukhtarullina A.R. Basic text category in translation: cognitive aspect of modality representation. Ufa: BashSU Publishing House, 2001.-132s.

67. I.S. Narskiy. Problems of meaning "value" in theory of cognition: // Problems of sign and value / edited by I.S. Narskiy. - M., 1969.

68. Nikitina S.E. Semantic analysis of science language. M., 1987.

69. Nuriakhmetova Yu.M. Method of determining the functional-cognitive potential of English verb-name phraseomatic combinations / Collection of scientific papers "Communicative and functional description of language". Ufa, BashSU, 2005.

70. Нуриахметова Ю.М. Концептуальная структура английских глагольноnamed phraseomatic combinations / Collection of scientific works "Communicative and functional description of language". Ufa, BashSU, 2005.

71. Nuriakhmetova Y.M. Frazeomatic significance and its conceptual организация (на материале английских verb-names

of phraseomatic combinations) // Bulletin of Bashkir University. Ufa: RIC BashSU, 2008. - №2. - C. 293-295.

72. Нуриахметова Ю.М. Сопоставление functional-cognitive Potential of English phraseomatic word combinations and their Russian equivalents in Oxford Russian Dictionary // Bulletin of Bashkir University. Ufa: BashSU Research Center, 2008. - №3. - C. 566-567.

73. Нуриахметова Ю.М. Лексикографическое представление функционально-когнитивного потенциала английских verb-names phraseomatic word combinations in English explanatory and English-Russian dictionaries. - Dis. ... cand. phil. - Ufa, 2008.

74. Popova Z.D. Semantic language space as a category of cognitive linguistics // Vestnik VSU. Series 1. Humanities. 1996, №2., c. 64-68.

75. Popova Z.D., Sternin I.A. Essays on cognitive linguistics. - Voronezh: Voronezh Un-ta Publishing House, 2002.

76. Richard J.F. Mental activity. Understanding, Reflection, Finding Solutions.

77. Рудакова Л.С. Конверсные соотношения между глаголом и глагольноname combination in English: Author's thesis .cand. phil. - M.-M.: 1980.

78. Rudenko S.A. Frazeo-lexical Verb Paradigm in Modern English: Authored Disc... cand. phil. of sciences. - M., 1981.

79. Ryabtseva N.K. "Question": Prototypical meaning of a concept // Logical language analysis: Cultural concepts. - Moscow; Nauka, 1991.

80. Sepir E. Selected works on linguistics and cultural studies. M.: 1993.

81. A.I. Smirnitsky to the question about the word (The problem of "separate words"). - M., 1952.

82. A.I. Smirnitsky English Lexicology. - Moscow: Lit. in English, 1956.

83. Stepanov Yu.S. Language and method: To the modern philosophy of language. - M.: 1998.

84. Telia V.N. Russian phraseology. Semantic, pragmatic and lingvocultural aspects. - Moscow: School of Russian Culture Languages, 1996.

85. Uralova L.A. Experience of Study of Stability of Phraseomatic Combinations: Autoref. Cand. phyll. sciences. - M.: 1979.

86. Fomina M.I. Modern Russian language. Lexicology. - M.,1983.

87. Cherdantseva T.Z. Idiomatics and Culture// The Polls of Linguistics 1996.- №1-
p.58-66.

88. Шанский   H.M.   Lexicology of modern Russian language.
Moscow: Prosv., 1972.

89. Щерба Л.В. Восточно-лужицкое наречие: Оттиск из записок историко-
philological fact of Petrogradsky Unta. - Petrograd, 1915. - T. I, XXIV.

90. Shcherba L.V. Experience of general theory of lexicography// Shcherba L.V.
Language system and speech activity. - Л.., 1974.

91. Shcherba L.V. Preface to the Great Russian-French Dictionary// Language system
and speech activity. - M.: Science, 1974.

92. Bally Ch. Precis de stylistique. - Geneve, 1905.

93. Felix S.W., Kanngiesser S., Rickheit G. 1990 - Preface / Language and
Knowledge: Studies in Cognitive Linguistics. - Opladen: Westdeutscher Verlag,
1990. pp. 1-3.

94. Jakendoff R. Conceptual semantics // U.Eco. M. Santambrogio,p. Violi.
Bloomington, 1988.-81p.

95. Linguistic Encyclopedic Dictionary / Ed. by V.N. Yartseva, - M.: Sov.
Encyclopedia, 1990. - 685 c.

96. Longman Dictionary of Contemporary English, The Pitman Press, 2001

97. New Webster's Dictionary of the English Language / Delhi, 1989.

I want morebooks!

Buy your books fast and straightforward online - at one of world's fastest growing online book stores! Environmentally sound due to Print-on-Demand technologies.

Buy your books online at
www.morebooks.shop

Kaufen Sie Ihre Bücher schnell und unkompliziert online – auf einer der am schnellsten wachsenden Buchhandelsplattformen weltweit! Dank Print-On-Demand umwelt- und ressourcenschonend produzi ert.

Bücher schneller online kaufen
www.morebooks.shop

KS OmniScriptum Publishing
Brivibas gatve 197
LV-1039 Riga, Latvia
Telefax: +371 686 204 55

info@omniscriptum.com
www.omniscriptum.com

OMNIScriptum

Printed by Books on Demand GmbH, Norderstedt / Germany

Mouhamadou Bamba Mboup

Como é que posso ganhar 1.000 dólares por dia online?

Mouhamadou Bamba Mboup

Como é que posso ganhar 1.000 dólares por dia online?

ScienciaScripts

Imprint
Any brand names and product names mentioned in this book are subject to trademark, brand or patent protection and are trademarks or registered trademarks of their respective holders. The use of brand names, product names, common names, trade names, product descriptions etc. even without a particular marking in this work is in no way to be construed to mean that such names may be regarded as unrestricted in respect of trademark and brand protection legislation and could thus be used by anyone.

Cover image: www.ingimage.com

This book is a translation from the original published under ISBN 978-620-6-71928-1.

Publisher:
Sciencia Scripts
is a trademark of
Dodo Books Indian Ocean Ltd. and OmniScriptum S.R.L publishing group

120 High Road, East Finchley, London, N2 9ED, United Kingdom
Str. Armeneasca 28/1, office 1, Chisinau MD-2012, Republic of Moldova, Europe
Printed at: see last page
ISBN: 978-620-7-98660-6

COMO É QUE POSSO GANHAR 1000 DÓLARES POR DIA NA INTERNET?

MOUHAMADOU BAMBA MBOUP

ÍNDICE

1. INTRODUÇÃO À GERAÇÃO DE RECEITAS EM LINHA

As vantagens de ganhar dinheiro na Internet

Ganhar dinheiro online tem uma série de vantagens que estão a atrair cada vez mais pessoas a explorar este caminho. Eis algumas das principais vantagens:

Flexibilidade: Uma das principais vantagens é a flexibilidade oferecida pelo trabalho em linha. Pode trabalhar a qualquer hora e em qualquer lugar, o que facilita o equilíbrio entre a sua vida profissional e pessoal.

Custos iniciais baixos: Ao contrário das empresas tradicionais, a criação de uma empresa em linha requer frequentemente um investimento mínimo. Pode começar com pouco ou nenhum dinheiro e desenvolver gradualmente o seu negócio.

Grande público-alvo: a Internet oferece acesso mundial a um grande público, o que significa que as suas oportunidades de rendimento não estão limitadas pela sua localização geográfica. Pode chegar a clientes de todo o mundo.

Diversidade de fontes de rendimento: Na Internet, há uma grande variedade de formas de ganhar dinheiro, seja através do marketing de afiliados, dropshipping, blogues ou criação e venda de produtos digitais. Esta diversidade permite-lhe explorar diferentes opções para maximizar o seu rendimento.

Potencial de crescimento ilimitado: Na Internet, não há limites para o rendimento que pode gerar. Com a estratégia correcta e muito esforço, pode aumentar consideravelmente os seus rendimentos ao longo do tempo. Estas vantagens tornam o trabalho em linha uma opção atractiva para quem procura aumentar o seu rendimento ou criar uma fonte alternativa de financiamento. Ao explorar as oportunidades oferecidas pela Internet, é possível atingir os seus objectivos financeiros e, ao mesmo tempo, desfrutar de maior liberdade e flexibilidade na sua vida profissional.

As diferentes formas de ganhar dinheiro online

Há uma grande variedade de métodos para gerar rendimentos em linha, cada um deles oferecendo oportunidades únicas e adaptadas a diferentes perfis empresariais. Eis algumas das principais formas de ganhar dinheiro em linha:

Marketing de afiliados: O marketing de afiliados envolve a promoção de produtos ou serviços de outras empresas e a obtenção de uma comissão sobre as vendas geradas pelos seus esforços promocionais. É um método popular porque não requer a criação de produtos ou a gestão de stocks.

Dropshipping: O Dropshipping é um modelo de negócio em que vende produtos sem ter de os armazenar fisicamente. Só efectua uma encomenda ao fornecedor quando recebe uma encomenda do seu cliente, o que reduz consideravelmente os custos iniciais.

Blogues: Os blogues são uma plataforma popular para gerar rendimentos em linha. Ao publicar conteúdos de qualidade e atrair um público fiel, pode rentabilizar o seu blogue através de publicidade, publicações patrocinadas ou venda de produtos digitais.

Venda de produtos digitais: Criar e vender produtos digitais, como livros electrónicos, cursos em linha ou software, pode ser uma fonte lucrativa de receitas em linha. Uma vez criado o produto, pode vendê-lo a um número ilimitado de clientes sem ter de suportar os custos associados à produção física.

Freelance: Trabalhar como freelancer em plataformas especializadas é outra forma de ganhar a vida online. Quer seja um redator, um designer gráfico, um programador Web ou um consultor, há uma procura crescente de serviços freelance em vários domínios.

Estes diferentes métodos oferecem aos empresários em linha a oportunidade de explorar várias fontes de rendimento e encontrar a que melhor se adapta às suas competências e objectivos financeiros. Combinando várias estratégias ou concentrando-se num único método, é possível criar um negócio rentável e sustentável na Internet.

As competências e os recursos necessários para ter êxito

A geração de receitas em linha requer um conjunto específico de competências e recursos para ter êxito neste domínio competitivo. Eis alguns elementos-chave a considerar:

Competências técnicas: Para ter sucesso em linha, é essencial dominar as ferramentas e plataformas digitais utilizadas para gerar receitas. Competências como a conceção de sítios Web, SEO, gestão de redes sociais e redação de conteúdos são essenciais para se destacar num ambiente digital.

Competências de marketing: Compreender os princípios do marketing em linha é crucial para atrair um público-alvo e converter visitantes em clientes pagantes. O conhecimento das estratégias de publicidade, da marca pessoal e da análise de dados pode fazer a diferença entre o sucesso e o fracasso de um negócio em linha.

Recursos financeiros: Embora alguns métodos de geração de rendimentos em linha exijam um investimento inicial reduzido, outros podem exigir recursos financeiros mais substanciais. É importante avaliar a sua capacidade financeira e planear um orçamento adequado para desenvolver o seu negócio em linha.

Criação de redes e colaboração: No mundo digital, a criação de redes com outros empresários em linha pode ser uma fonte valiosa de oportunidades e apoio. A colaboração com parceiros ou influenciadores também pode ajudar a aumentar a sua visibilidade e credibilidade na Internet. Para ter êxito na geração de receitas em linha, é essencial desenvolver um conjunto diversificado de competências técnicas, de marketing e interpessoais. Combinando estas competências com recursos financeiros bem geridos e uma rede forte, os empresários podem maximizar as suas hipóteses de sucesso neste dinâmico mundo digital.

Referências:

https://www.lesaffaires.com/blogues/stephanie-leroux/gagner-sa-vie-sur-internet-les- cles-du-succes/611013

https://www.blogdumoderateur.com/reussir-business-en-ligne/
https://www.journaldunet.com/web-tech/dictionnaire-du-webmastering/1209341-passive-income-definition-and-examples/:~:text=A%20passive%20income%20is%20a,of%20fa%C3%A7on%20r%C3

2. MARKETING DE AFILIAÇÃO

Compreender o marketing de afiliação e o seu funcionamento

O marketing de afiliados é um método popular de gerar rendimentos em linha que envolve a promoção de produtos ou serviços de outras empresas. A essência do marketing de afiliação é que os afiliados recebem uma comissão por cada venda ou ação gerada através dos seus esforços promocionais. Esta abordagem permite aos afiliados ganhar dinheiro sem terem de criar ou gerir produtos, o que a torna uma opção atractiva para muitos empresários em linha. O marketing de afiliação funciona com base numa parceria entre o anunciante (a empresa que oferece o produto ou serviço) e o afiliado (o promotor). Quando um afiliado decide promover um produto específico, recebe uma ligação única, denominada ligação de afiliado, que lhe permite acompanhar as vendas e as acções geradas pela sua promoção. Sempre que um utilizador clica nesta ligação e efectua uma compra ou realiza uma ação desejada, o afiliado recebe uma comissão pré-determinada. Para ter êxito no marketing de afiliação, é essencial que os afiliados escolham produtos ou serviços que sejam relevantes para o seu público-alvo. O conhecimento profundo do seu público e das suas necessidades é crucial para criar conteúdos persuasivos e eficazes. Além disso, os afiliados devem utilizar vários canais de promoção, como blogues, redes sociais, boletins informativos ou mesmo publicidade paga, para maximizar a sua visibilidade e aumentar as suas hipóteses de conversão. Os afiliados devem revelar claramente a sua relação com o anunciante, a fim de criar confiança junto do seu público. Respeitando estes princípios fundamentais e aplicando estratégias eficazes, os afiliados podem tirar o máximo partido do potencial lucrativo do marketing de afiliação, oferecendo simultaneamente um valor acrescentado aos seus seguidores.

Encontre os melhores programas de afiliação para maximizar os seus ganhos

Um passo crucial no marketing de afiliação é encontrar os programas que oferecem as melhores oportunidades de ganho. Eis algumas dicas para escolher os melhores programas de afiliação:

Pesquisa aprofundada: Reserve algum tempo para pesquisar e analisar diferentes programas de afiliação no seu nicho. Compare as comissões oferecidas, as condições de pagamento, a reputação do anunciante e a qualidade dos produtos ou serviços oferecidos.

Adequação ao seu público: Escolha programas que correspondam aos interesses e necessidades do seu público-alvo. Opte por produtos ou serviços que despertem o interesse dos seus seguidores e aumentem as suas hipóteses de conversão.

Reputação do anunciante: Trabalhar com anunciantes fiáveis e bem estabelecidos pode garantir pagamentos atempados e uma colaboração frutuosa. Procure aconselhamento sobre o anunciante antes de se comprometer com um programa de afiliação.

Ferramentas e apoio: Certifique-se de que o programa de afiliação oferece ferramentas de marketing eficazes, como banners, hiperligações controladas e conteúdos promocionais. Um bom apoio ao cliente é também essencial para responder às suas perguntas e ajudá-lo a otimizar as suas campanhas.

Potencial de ganhos: Avalie o potencial de ganhos oferecido por cada programa em termos de taxa de comissão, volume de vendas previsto e montante médio por transação. Escolha programas que ofereçam um equilíbrio entre rentabilidade e viabilidade. Ao seguir estes conselhos, poderá identificar os melhores programas de afiliação para maximizar os seus ganhos. Não se esqueça de que a qualidade é mais importante do que a quantidade. É preferível promover com sucesso alguns produtos ou serviços relevantes do que distribuir os seus esforços por uma multiplicidade de ofertas de fraco desempenho.

Utilizar estratégias eficazes para promover produtos e gerar vendas

Depois de ter selecionado os melhores programas de afiliação, é essencial utilizar estratégias eficazes para promover os produtos e aumentar as suas hipóteses de gerar vendas. Eis algumas dicas para maximizar o seu sucesso como afiliado:

Criar conteúdo de qualidade: Criar conteúdo relevante e cativante é essencial para atrair a atenção do seu público. Quer seja através de artigos de blogue, vídeos, podcasts ou publicações nas redes sociais, certifique-se de que fornece conteúdo informativo que realça as vantagens do produto que está a promover.

Utilizar o marketing por correio eletrónico: O marketing por correio eletrónico continua a ser uma das formas mais eficazes de promover produtos de afiliados. Crie uma lista de subscritores qualificados e envie-lhes regularmente boletins informativos personalizados com ofertas especiais e recomendações de produtos.

Otimizar as referências: Certifique-se de que o seu conteúdo é bem referenciado nos motores de busca para atrair tráfego orgânico para as suas ligações de afiliado. Utilize palavras-chave relevantes, crie backlinks de qualidade e optimize a estrutura do seu sítio Web para melhorar a sua visibilidade online.

Colaborar com outros influenciadores: A parceria com outros influenciadores do seu nicho pode ajudá-lo a alargar o seu alcance e a atingir um público mais vasto. Ao trabalharem em conjunto em campanhas promocionais ou ao partilharem o seu conteúdo uns com os outros, podem beneficiar da sua credibilidade e do seu público já estabelecido.

Acompanhe e analise o seu desempenho: Utilize ferramentas de análise para acompanhar o seu desempenho em termos de cliques, conversões e receitas geradas.

Identifique o que funciona melhor para si e ajuste as suas estratégias em conformidade para maximizar os seus resultados.

Ao implementar estas estratégias eficazes, poderá promover produtos de afiliados com sucesso e aumentar as suas hipóteses de gerar vendas lucrativas. O envolvimento constante com o seu público, a otimização contínua dos seus esforços de marketing e a colaboração inteligente com outros intervenientes-chave são fundamentais para o sucesso do marketing de afiliação.

Referências:

https://www.blogdumoderateur.com/strategies-marketing-affiliation/https://www.webmarketing-conseil.fr/comment-promouvoir-produits-affiliation/
https://www.markentive.fr/blog/marketing-daffiliation-strategies-reussir/

3. DROPSHIPPING

3.1 O que é o dropshipping e como funciona?

O dropshipping é um modelo de negócio cada vez mais popular que permite aos empresários vender produtos sem ter de gerir o inventário ou a expedição. Ao contrário do comércio eletrónico tradicional, em que o vendedor tem de comprar e armazenar os produtos que vende, o dropshipping implica que o fornecedor envie os produtos diretamente para o cliente final em nome do vendedor.

O Dropshipping funciona de uma forma relativamerte simples. O empresário cria uma loja em linha para vender produtos fornecidos por grossistas ou fabricantes. Quando um cliente faz uma encomenda na loja em linha, o vendedor reencaminha a encomenda para o fornecedor, que depois envia o produto diretamente para o cliente. O vendedor nunca manuseia fisicamente os produtos, o que reduz consideravelmente os custos associados à gestão das existências e à expedição.

Um aspeto fundamental do dropshipping é a margem de lucro obtida pelo vendedor. Ao fixar um preço de venda mais elevaco do que o preço de compra acordado com o fornecedor, o vendedor pode gerar lucros sem ter de investir no stock inicial. No entanto, é essencial encontrar um equilíbrio entre a fixação de um preço atrativo para os clientes e a obtenção de margens de lucro suficientes para manter a rentabilidade da empresa.

Além disso, o sucesso do dropshipping depende da seleção de

bons fornecedores e de produtos rentáveis. Trabalhar com parceiros fiáveis que ofereçam uma qualidade consistente e prazos de entrega rápidos é crucial para garantir a satisfação do cliente. Além disso, a escolha de produtos populares e procurados pelo seu público-alvo pode aumentar as suas hipóteses de sucesso com este modelo de negócio. Em suma, o dropshipping oferece aos empresários uma oportunidade única de criar um negócio online sem os tradicionais constrangimentos logísticos. Ao compreender como funciona este modelo de negócio e ao implementar uma estratégia eficaz baseada em parcerias sólidas e numa seleção criteriosa de produtos, é possível tirar o máximo partido do potencial lucrativo do dropshipping.

3.2 Encontre os melhores fornecedores e produtos para iniciar o seu negócio de dropshipping

Quando lança o seu negócio de dropshipping, encontrar os fornecedores e produtos certos é essencial para o sucesso do seu negócio online. A seleção dos parceiros certos pode ter um impacto significativo na qualidade dos produtos, na satisfação dos clientes e na rentabilidade global da sua empresa. Para encontrar os melhores fornecedores, é aconselhável efetuar uma pesquisa exaustiva e avaliar vários critérios-chave. Certifique-se de que os seus potenciais fornecedores oferecem uma qualidade de produto consistente, prazos de entrega rápidos e um bom serviço ao cliente. Pode consultar plataformas online especializadas em dropshipping para descobrir novos fornecedores ou contactar diretamente os fabricantes para estabelecer parcerias sólidas. No que diz respeito à escolha dos produtos, é importante selecionar artigos que sejam populares e procurados pelo seu público-alvo. Analise as tendências do mercado, identifique as necessidades não satisfeitas e ofereça uma gama variada de produtos atractivos para atrair um vasto leque de potenciais clientes. Deve também certificar-se de que estabelece preços competitivos, preservando simultaneamente as suas margens de lucro para garantir a viabilidade financeira da sua empresa. Outra estratégia eficaz consiste em testar diferentes fornecedores e produtos antes de tomar decisões finais. Lance campanhas-piloto, analise o desempenho de cada produto e avalie a capacidade de resposta e a fiabilidade dos seus fornecedores em situações reais. Esta abordagem permitir-lhe-á otimizar o seu catálogo de produtos e estabelecer relações duradouras com parceiros de confiança.Em conclusão, encontrar os melhores fornecedores e produtos para iniciar o seu negócio dropshipping requer tempo, pesquisa e uma abordagem estratégica. Ao investir na seleção cuidadosa dos seus parceiros comerciais e ao oferecer uma gama atraente de produtos rentáveis, pode posicionar a sua empresa para o sucesso no mundo competitivo do comércio eletrónico.

3.3 Criar uma loja virtual eficaz e otimizar as vendas

Depois de ter encontrado os melhores fornecedores e produtos para o seu negócio de dropshipping, é essencial criar uma loja online eficaz para maximizar as suas vendas. Uma boa conceção do sítio Web e uma estratégia de marketing sólida podem fazer a diferença entre o sucesso e o fracasso da sua empresa.

Para começar, certifique-se de que o seu sítio Web é de fácil utilização, intuitivo e profissional. Escolha um design atrativo que destaque os seus produtos, facilite a navegação dos clientes e incentive a compra por impulso. Certifique-se de que a sua loja virtual está optimizada para dispositivos móveis, uma vez que são cada vez mais os compradores que fazem compras em smartphones e tablets.

Em seguida, desenvolva uma estratégia de marketing abrangente para atrair tráfego para o seu sítio Web. Utilize técnicas como a otimização dos motores de busca (SEO), a publicidade paga (Google Ads, Facebook Ads), o marketing por correio eletrónico e as redes sociais para promover os seus produtos junto de um vasto público. Analise regularmente o desempenho das suas campanhas de marketing para ajustar a sua estratégia e maximizar o retorno do investimento.

Depois de ter atraído visitantes para o seu sítio Web, certifique-se de que optimiza o processo de compra para aumentar as suas taxas de conversão. Simplifique o processo de encomenda, ofereça opções de pagamento seguras e forneça um serviço de apoio ao cliente reativo para tranquilizar os potenciais clientes. Utilize ferramentas de análise da Web para acompanhar o comportamento dos utilizadores no seu sítio e identificar as áreas a melhorar. Finalmente, não se esqueça da importância do serviço pós-venda para manter os clientes actuais e encorajar recomendações positivas. Ofereça um apoio ao cliente de qualidade, trate rapidamente quaisquer devoluções ou problemas com que os clientes se deparem e procure constantemente melhorar a experiência global de compra na sua loja em linha.

Ao combinar uma loja virtual bem concebida com uma estratégia de marketing eficaz e um serviço ao cliente excecional, pode maximizar as suas vendas de dropshipping e construir um negócio de comércio eletrónico de sucesso.

Referências:

https://www.oberlo.fr/blog/strategie-marketing-dropshipping
https://www.shopify.fr/guides/dropshipping
https://www.ecommerce-nation.fr/optimiser-votre-boutique-en-ligne-pour-le- dropshipping/

4. CRIAR CONTEÚDOS RENTÁVEIS

4.1 Identificar os tipos de conteúdos que geram receitas na .

Identificar os tipos de conteúdos rentáveis é essencial para os criadores de conteúdos em linha que procuram maximizar as suas receitas. Diferentes formatos de conteúdos podem ser rentabilizados de diferentes formas e é crucial compreender quais os tipos de conteúdos mais rentáveis num determinado contexto.

Os vídeos patrocinados são um dos tipos de conteúdo mais lucrativos para muitos criadores. As parcerias com marcas para promover os seus produtos ou serviços em vídeos podem gerar receitas significativas através de colaborações pagas. Do mesmo modo, os artigos patrocinados oferecem uma oportunidade semelhante para os bloguistas e influenciadores serem pagos para escrever sobre marcas ou produtos específicos.

As publicações nas redes sociais também podem ser uma importante fonte de receitas em linha. Os influenciadores com uma forte presença em plataformas como o Instagram, o TikTok ou o YouTube podem trabalhar com marcas para criar conteúdos patrocinados ou promover produtos junto do seu público. Estas parcerias pagas podem ser extremamente lucrativas para os criadores com uma base de subscritores empenhada.

Além disso, a criação e a venda de produtos digitais, como livros electrónicos, cursos em linha ou modelos gráficos, podem constituir uma fonte estável de receitas em linha. Os criadores talentosos podem rentabilizar a sua experiência oferecendo conteúdos exclusivos a um público disposto a pagar pelo acesso a estes recursos especializados.

Por último, o marketing de afiliados é outra estratégia popular para gerar receitas em linha através de conteúdos. Ao recomendar produtos ou serviços de terceiros através de ligações de afiliados, os criadores podem ganhar uma comissão por cada venda efectuada em resultado da sua recomendação. Esta abordagem pode ser particularmente lucrativa se o criador tiver um público fiel e empenhado pronto a seguir as suas recomendações.Em conclusão, a identificação dos tipos de conteúdo que geram receitas em linha requer uma compreensão profunda do mercado e do público-alvo. Ao escolher sabiamente entre as diferentes opções disponíveis e ao desenvolver uma estratégia adaptada à sua área de especialização, um criador pode explorar plenamente o potencial financeiro oferecido pela criação de conteúdos lucrativos na Internet.

4.2 Criar conteúdos de qualidade que atraiam o seu público-alvo

Criar conteúdos de qualidade é essencial para atrair e reter um público-alvo. Compreender as necessidades, os interesses e as preferências do seu público é crucial para produzir conteúdos relevantes e cativantes.

Uma abordagem eficaz consiste em efetuar uma análise aprofundada do seu público para identificar os temas que suscitam mais interesse. Utilizando ferramentas de análise das redes sociais ou inquéritos, pode recolher dados valiosos sobre as preferências do seu público e adaptar o seu conteúdo em conformidade.

Além disso, diversificar o formato do conteúdo pode ajudar a atrair uma vasta gama de públicos. Para além dos artigos escritos, considere a possibilidade de integrar vídeos, infográficos, podcasts ou mesmo webinars para oferecer uma experiência variada aos seus subscritores.

Outro aspeto importante é a regularidade com que o conteúdo é publicado. Ao manter uma cadência regular e previsível, pode fidelizar o seu público, fornecendo-lhe um fluxo constante de novas informações e reforçando a sua confiança na sua marca.

Por último, não se esqueça da importância da interação com o seu público. Responda aos comentários, faça perguntas para incentivar a participação e criar um sentido de comunidade em torno do seu conteúdo. Isto não só aumentará a lealdade do seu público, como também atrairá novos subscritores através do boca-a-boca positivo. Em conclusão, a criação de conteúdos de qualidade que atraiam o seu público-alvo exige um conhecimento profundo das suas necessidades e preferências. Ao adaptar a sua estratégia editorial de acordo com o feedback do seu público e ao encorajar a interação e o envolvimento, pode maximizar o impacto do seu conteúdo e aumentar a sua rentabilidade a longo prazo.

4.3 Rentabilizar os conteúdos através de publicidade, parcerias e produtos digitais

Quando se trata de rentabilizar o seu conteúdo, há uma série de estratégias eficazes que podem ajudá-lo a gerar receitas e, ao mesmo tempo, oferecer valor acrescentado ao seu público. A publicidade, as parcerias e os produtos digitais são formas populares de rentabilizar os seus conteúdos.

A publicidade é uma das formas mais comuns de gerar receitas a partir do seu conteúdo. Pode incorporar anúncios no seu sítio Web, vídeos ou podcasts para chegar a uma vasta audiência e ganhar dinheiro com base no número de visualizações ou cliques. É essencial escolher anunciantes que sejam relevantes para o seu público, a fim de maximizar os seus ganhos e manter os seus subscritores envolvidos.

As parcerias com outras marcas ou influenciadores também podem ser uma fonte interessante de receitas. Ao colaborar com empresas que partilham os seus valores, pode criar conteúdos patrocinados ou promoções cruzadas que beneficiam tanto o seu público como os seus parceiros. Certifique-se de que estas colaborações são transparentes e genuínas para manter a confiança do seu público.

Por último, a criação e venda de produtos digitais pode ser outra fonte sustentável de receitas. Quer se trate de livros electrónicos, cursos em linha, ferramentas digitais ou mesmo de subscrições premium, a oferta de conteúdos exclusivos e de elevado valor acrescentado pode incentivar o seu público a investir nos seus produtos. Certifique-se de que promove estes produtos estrategicamente no seu conteúdo para maximizar a sua visibilidade e atração.

Combinando judiciosamente a publicidade, as parcerias e os produtos digitais, pode diversificar as suas fontes de rendimento, oferecendo simultaneamente conteúdos enriquecedores e relevantes ao seu público-alvo. Esta abordagem proactiva pode ajudá-lo não só a rentabilizar os seus conteúdos, mas também a reforçar a fidelidade dos seus assinantes a longo prazo.

Referências:

https://www.blogdumoderateur.com/monetiser-contenu-digital/
https://www.lesechos.fr/idees-debats/cercle/opinion-comment-monetiser-son-contenu-sur-internet-1313666
https://www.journaldunet.com/web-tech/dictionnaire-du-webmastering/1445724-monetisation-definition-and-strategies-for-making-money-with-a-website/

5. GESTÃO EFICAZ DO TEMPO E DOS RECURSOS

5.1 Planear as suas actividades em linha para maximizar a sua produtividade

Quando se trata de gerir eficazmente o tempo e os recursos em linha, o planeamento de actividades desempenha um papel crucial na maximização da produtividade. Ao estabelecer um calendário claro e estruturado, os indivíduos podem organizar as suas tarefas de forma estratégica para maximizar a sua eficiência.

O primeiro passo consiste em identificar as prioridades e os objectivos a atingir. Ao definir claramente o que tem de ser feito, torna-se mais fácil afetar tempo e recursos de forma adequada. Desta forma, evita-se a procrastinação e permite-se concentrar nas tarefas essenciais para progredir em direção aos objectivos. Em seguida, é importante elaborar um calendário realista, tendo em conta os condicionalismos pessoais e profissionais. Ao atribuir a cada atividade um período de tempo específico, torna-se mais fácil manter a disciplina e a regularidade na execução das tarefas planeadas.

A utilização de ferramentas de gestão do tempo em linha também pode ser benéfica para um planeamento eficaz. Aplicações como o Trello, o Asana ou o Google Calendar oferecem funcionalidades para organizar tarefas, estabelecer prazos e acompanhar a evolução dos projectos em tempo real.

Por último, incluir intervalos e tempo de recuperação no seu horário é essencial para evitar o esgotamento e manter níveis óptimos de produtividade. Tirar tempo para descansar e recarregar as baterias pode melhorar a concentração e a criatividade quando regressa ao trabalho.

Em conclusão, o planeamento rigoroso e metódico das suas actividades em linha é um fator essencial para maximizar a sua produtividade. Ao adotar uma abordagem proactiva para organizar o seu tempo e utilizar as ferramentas certas, pode otimizar a utilização dos recursos disponíveis para atingir com êxito os seus objectivos.

5.2 Utilizar ferramentas e técnicas para otimizar o seu tempo e os seus recursos

Quando se trata de otimizar o tempo e os recursos, a utilização das ferramentas e técnicas correctas pode facilitar muito a gestão eficaz das actividades. Ao incorporar estes elementos no seu planeamento, pode maximizar a produtividade e atingir os seus objectivos de forma mais eficiente.

Utilizar aplicações de gestão do tempo: Aplicações como o Trello, Asana, Todoist ou Google Calendar oferecem uma série de funcionalidades para organizar tarefas, estabelecer prazos, partilhar projectos de equipa e acompanhar os progressos em tempo real. Estas ferramentas proporcionam uma melhor visão geral das actividades a realizar e ajudam-no a dar prioridade às tarefas de acordo com a sua importância e urgência.

Técnicas de gestão do tempo: A técnica Pomodoro, baseada em intervalos de trabalho concentrado seguidos de pequenas pausas, pode ajudar a manter a concentração, evitando a fadiga mental. Do mesmo modo, o método Eisenhower, que consiste em classificar as tarefas de acordo com a sua urgência e importância, ajuda-o a organizar melhor o seu tempo, concentrando-se nas actividades essenciais.

Externalizar tarefas não prioritárias: Para aproveitar ao máximo o seu tempo, é por vezes uma boa ideia subcontratar certas tarefas não essenciais. Recorrer a um assistente virtual ou delegar responsabilidades pode libertar tempo para se concentrar nas actividades essenciais que precisam de atenção.

Estas ferramentas e técnicas são úteis não só para gerir o tempo, mas também para otimizar a utilização dos recursos disponíveis. Ao combinar um planeamento rigoroso com a integração adequada de ferramentas digitais e métodos comprovados, é possível melhorar significativamente a eficiência na realização das tarefas diárias.

Evitar as armadilhas comuns da gestão do tempo e dos recursos em linha

Quando se trata de gerir eficazmente o seu tempo e recursos em linha, é crucial evitar certas armadilhas comuns que podem prejudicar a produtividade e o sucesso. Ao identificar estes potenciais obstáculos, pode contorná-los e melhorar significativamente a sua gestão do tempo e dos recursos.

Sobrecarga de informação: Uma das principais armadilhas em linha é a superabundância de informação disponível, que pode levar a que se perca tempo a navegar entre diferentes fontes sem que se concluam efetivamente tarefas importantes. É essencial definir objectivos claros e limitar o consumo de informações irrelevantes para se manter concentrado nas tarefas prioritárias.

Distrações digitais: As distracções em linha, como as notificações incessantes das redes sociais, os e-mails não urgentes ou a navegação em sítios Web não profissionais, podem afetar significativamente a gestão do tempo. É aconselhável reservar períodos específicos sem interrupções para se poder concentrar totalmente nas tarefas importantes.

Utilização incorrecta das ferramentas digitais: Embora as ferramentas digitais possam ser extremamente úteis para otimizar a gestão do tempo, a sua má utilização também pode ser uma armadilha. É essencial escolher as aplicações correctas para as suas necessidades específicas e não se deixar dominar por uma multiplicidade de ferramentas inúteis que complicam em vez de ajudar.

Ao evitar estas armadilhas comuns da gestão do tempo e dos recursos em linha, pode maximizar a sua eficiência e produtividade. Se estiver atento a estes potenciais obstáculos e adotar estratégias para os contornar, é mais fácil atingir os seus objectivos profissionais, mantendo um equilíbrio saudável entre a sua vida pessoal e profissional.

Referências:

Artigo sobre a gestão do tempo e dos recursos em online-
www.exemple.com/gestion-temps-en-ligne

Guia para evitar as distracções digitais-
www.exemple.com/distractions-numeriques

Livro sobre a otimização da produtividade com as ferramentas
digitais - www.exemple.com/productivite-outils-numeriques

6. PERSEVERANÇA E CRIATIVIDADE PARA TER SUCESSO NA INTERNET

6.1 Cultivar uma mentalidade de sucesso e ultrapassar obstáculos

O sucesso online não depende apenas de competências técnicas, mas também de uma mentalidade positiva e perseverante. Cultivar uma mentalidade de sucesso significa acreditar nas suas capacidades, ser resiliente perante os contratempos e manter-se motivado apesar dos obstáculos que encontra.

Para ultrapassar obstáculos, é essencial definir objectivos claros e exequíveis. Ter uma visão clara do que se pretende alcançar facilita a concentração e a determinação. Além disso, aprender a transformar os contratempos em oportunidades de aprendizagem significa que pode recuperar mais rapidamente e avançar para o sucesso.

A perseverança desempenha um papel crucial na concretização dos objectivos em linha. Face a desafios e contratempos, é importante manter a motivação e continuar a avançar apesar das dificuldades. A capacidade de persistir nos seus esforços, de se adaptar à mudança e de enfrentar os desafios com determinação são qualidades essenciais para o sucesso em linha.

Além disso, é essencial desenvolver uma atitude proactiva face aos obstáculos. Em vez de se deixar desencorajar pelas dificuldades encontradas, é necessário adotar uma abordagem construtiva, procurando soluções alternativas e mantendo-se aberto às mudanças necessárias para progredir em direção aos seus objectivos.

Concluindo, cultivar uma mentalidade de sucesso e ultrapassar obstáculos é a chave para o sucesso online. Ao adotar uma atitude positiva, perseverante e proactiva, é possível enfrentar os desafios com confiança e determinação, abrindo caminho para o sucesso profissional na Internet.

6.2 Encontrar soluções criativas para se destacar num mercado competitivo

Num ambiente em linha saturado e competitivo, é essencial encontrar soluções criativas para se destacar da multidão e atrair a atenção de potenciais clientes. A criatividade pode ser um trunfo importante para as empresas que procuram posicionar-se de forma única no mercado.

Uma abordagem inovadora pode assumir muitas formas, desde a conceção de produtos originais à implementação de campanhas de marketing inovadoras e à criação de uma experiência excecional para o cliente. Ao ultrapassar os limites tradicionais e pensar fora da caixa, uma empresa pode cativar o seu público-alvo e diferenciar-se dos seus concorrentes.

A criatividade não se limita apenas ao domínio do design ou do marketing; pode também estender-se à forma como uma empresa aborda os seus processos internos. Ao adotar formas inovadoras de trabalhar, como o teletrabalho flexível, a colaboração interdisciplinar ou a integração de tecnologias disruptivas, uma empresa pode não só melhorar a sua eficiência operacional como também reforçar a sua posição no mercado.

A criatividade também pode ser vista na forma como uma empresa comunica com o seu público. Ao utilizar as redes sociais de forma original, ao lançar campanhas virais ou ao oferecer conteúdos interessantes e divertidos, uma empresa pode despertar o interesse e o empenho da sua comunidade em linha.

Em conclusão, encontrar soluções criativas para se destacar num mercado competitivo é essencial para o sucesso em linha. Ao cultivar um espírito de inovação e explorar constantemente novas ideias e abordagens, uma empresa pode não só sobreviver num ambiente competitivo, mas também prosperar e crescer de forma sustentável na Internet.

6.3 Adaptar-se à mudança e aproveitar as oportunidades para continuar a gerar receitas

A capacidade de adaptação às rápidas mudanças no mercado em linha é crucial para manter a viabilidade de uma empresa e continuar a gerar receitas. As empresas que se mantêm fixas correm o risco de serem ultrapassadas pela concorrência e de perderem quota de mercado. Por isso, é essencial manter-se ágil e flexível para aproveitar as oportunidades que vão surgindo. Uma estratégia eficaz para se adaptar à mudança é manter-se atento às tendências do mercado, ao comportamento dos consumidores e aos desenvolvimentos tecnológicos. Ao manter-se constantemente informada, uma empresa pode antecipar futuras mudanças e ajustar a sua estratégia em conformidade. Por exemplo, se uma nova plataforma de redes sociais ganhar popularidade, a empresa deve estar preparada para investir tempo e recursos nessa plataforma para atingir um novo público. Além disso, é importante incentivar uma cultura de inovação na empresa, para que os funcionários sejam encorajados a apresentar ideias inovadoras em resposta aos desafios do mercado em constante mudança. A criatividade e a colaboração podem levar a soluções únicas que permitem à empresa destacar-se e manter-se relevante. Finalmente, aproveitar as oportunidades para continuar a gerar receitas também significa ser proactivo na procura de novas fontes de rendimento. Isto pode implicar o desenvolvimento de novos produtos ou serviços, a exploração de parcerias estratégicas ou mesmo a diversificação dos canais de venda em linha. Ao estar constantemente à procura de oportunidades de expansão, uma empresa pode garantir o seu crescimento contínuo no mercado digital. Em conclusão, a adaptação à mudança e o aproveitamento de oportunidades são fundamentais para manter a competitividade e a rentabilidade de um negócio em linha. Ao adotar uma abordagem proactiva e ao promover a inovação, uma empresa pode não só sobreviver num ambiente dinâmico, mas também prosperar a longo prazo.

Referências:

32

Smith, J. (2020). Como se adaptar às rápidas mudanças no mercado online. Harvard Business Review.

Dupont, A. (2019). A importância da inovação para capturar oportunidades de receita. Journal of Business Strategy.

Gagnon, C. et al. (2018). Estratégias de crescimento para negócios online. Revista internacional de gestão e economia.

RESUMO DO LIVRO

Pode trabalhar a qualquer hora e em qualquer lugar, o que facilita o equilíbrio entre a sua vida profissional e pessoal. Pode começar com pouco ou nenhum dinheiro e desenvolver gradualmente o seu negócio. Pode chegar a clientes de todo o mundo. Estas vantagens fazem do trabalho em linha uma opção atractiva para quem procura aumentar o seu rendimento ou criar uma fonte alternativa de financiamento. Ao explorar as oportunidades oferecidas pela Internet, é possível atingir os seus objectivos financeiros e, ao mesmo tempo, desfrutar de maior liberdade e flexibilidade na sua vida profissional. Existem inúmeros métodos para gerar rendimentos em linha, cada um oferecendo oportunidades únicas e adaptadas a diferentes perfis empresariais.

As diferentes formas de ganhar dinheiro online

Trata-se de um método popular porque não exige a criação de produtos nem a gestão de stocks. Ao publicar conteúdos de qualidade e atrair um público fiel, pode rentabilizar o seu blogue através de publicidade, publicações patrocinadas cu venda de produtos digitais. Uma vez criado o produto, pode vendê-lo a um número ilimitado de clientes sem ter de suportar os custos associados à produção física. Quer seja um redator, um designer gráfico, um programador Web ou um consultor, há uma procura crescente de serviços freelance em vários domínios. Estes diferentes métodos oferecem aos empresários online a oportunidade de explorar várias fontes de rendimento e encontrar a que melhor se adequa às suas competências e objectivos financeiros. Combinando várias estratégias ou concentrando-se num único método, é possível criar um negócio online rentável e sustentável. A geração de rendimentos em linha requer um conjunto específico de competências e recursos para ter êxito neste domínio competitivo.

As competências e os recursos necessários para ter êxito

Competências como a conceção de sítios Web, SEO, gestão de redes sociais e redação de conteúdos são essenciais para se destacar num ambiente digital. O conhecimento das estratégias de publicidade, da marca pessoal e da análise de dados pode fazer a diferença entre o sucesso e o fracasso de um negócio em linha. É importante avaliar as suas capacidades financeiras e planear um orçamento adequado para desenvolver o seu negócio em linha. Para ter êxito na geração de receitas em linha, é essencial desenvolver um conjunto diversificado de competências técnicas, de marketing e interpessoais. Ao combinar estas competências com recursos financeiros bem geridos e uma rede de contactos forte, os empresários podem maximizar as suas hipóteses de sucesso neste mundo digital dinâmico.

Encontre os melhores programas de afiliação para maximizar os seus ganhos

Compare as comissões oferecidas, as condições de pagamento, a reputação do anunciante e a qualidade dos produtos ou serviços oferecidos. Opte por produtos ou serviços que despertem o interesse dos seus seguidores e aumentem as suas hipóteses de conversão. Procure opiniões sobre o anunciante antes de se comprometer com um programa de afiliação. Um bom apoio ao cliente é também essencial para responder às suas questões e ajudá-lo a otimizar as suas campanhas. Seguindo estes conselhos, poderá identificar os melhores programas de afiliação para maximizar os seus ganhos. Lembre-se que a qualidade é mais importante do que a quantidade, por isso é melhor promover alguns produtos ou serviços relevantes com sucesso do que espalhar os seus esforços por uma multidão de ofertas de baixo desempenho. Depois de ter selecionado os melhores programas de afiliação, é essencial utilizar estratégias eficazes para promover os produtos e aumentar as suas hipóteses de gerar vendas.

Utilizar estratégias eficazes para promover produtos e gerar vendas

Quer seja através de artigos de blogue, vídeos, podcasts ou publicações nas redes sociais, certifique-se de que fornece conteúdos informativos que realçam as vantagens do produto que está a promover. Utilize palavras-chave relevantes, crie backlinks de qualidade e optimize a estrutura do seu sítio Web para melhorar a sua visibilidade em linha. Ao trabalharem em conjunto em campanhas promocionais ou ao partilharem o seu conteúdo, pode beneficiar da credibilidade e do público estabelecido dos seus parceiros. Identifique o que funciona melhor para si e ajuste as suas estratégias em conformidade para maximizar os seus resultados.

Ao implementar estas estratégias eficazes, será capaz de promover produtos de afiliados com sucesso e aumentar as suas hipóteses de gerar vendas. lucrativas. O envolvimento constante com o seu público, a otimização contínua dos seus esforços de marketing e a colaboração inteligente com outros intervenientes-chave são fundamentais para o sucesso no marketing de afiliados. O dropshipping é um modelo de negócio cada vez mais popular que permite aos empresários venderem produtos sem terem de gerir o inventário ou a expedição. Ao contrário do comércio eletrónico tradicional, em que o vendedor tem de comprar e armazenar os produtos que vende, o dropshipping implica que o fornecedor envie os produtos diretamente para o cliente final em nome do vendedor.

O Dropshipping funciona de uma forma relativamente simples. O empresário cria uma loja em linha para vender produtos fornecidos por grossistas ou fabricantes. Quando um cliente faz uma encomenda na loja em linha, o vendedor reencaminha a encomenda para o fornecedor, que, por sua vez, envia o produto diretamente para o cliente. Um aspeto fundamental do dropshipping é a margem de lucro obtida pelo vendedor. Além disso, o êxito do dropshipping depende da seleção de bons fornecedores e de produtos rentáveis. Em suma, o dropshipping oferece aos empresários uma oportunidade única de criar um negócio online sem os tradicionais constrangimentos logísticos. Ao compreender o funcionamento deste modelo de negócio e ao pôr em prática uma estratégia eficaz baseada em parcerias sólidas e numa seleção criteriosa dos produtos, é possível tirar o máximo partido do potencial lucrativo do dropshipping.

Encontre os melhores fornecedores e produtos para iniciar o seu negócio de dropshipping

Quando lançar o seu negócio de dropshipping, encontrar os fornecedores e produtos certos é essencial para o sucesso do seu negócio online. Pode consultar plataformas em linha especializadas em dropshipping para descobrir novos fornecedores ou contactar diretamente os fabricantes para estabelecer parcerias sólidas. No que diz respeito à escolha dos produtos, é importante selecionar artigos que sejam populares e procurados pelo seu público-alvo. Em conclusão, encontrar os melhores fornecedores e produtos para iniciar o seu negócio de dropshipping requer tempo, investigação e uma abordagem estratégica. Depois de ter encontrado os melhores fornecedores e produtos para o seu negócio de dropshipping, é essencial criar uma loja online eficaz para maximizar as suas vendas. Uma boa conceção do sítio Web e uma estratégia de marketing sólida podem fazer a diferença entre o sucesso e o fracasso da sua empresa. Certifique-se de que a sua loja virtual está optimizada para dispositivos móveis, uma vez que são cada vez mais os compradores que fazem compras em smartphones e tablets. Utilize técnicas como a otimização dos motores de busca, a publicidade paga, o marketing por correio eletrónico e as redes sociais para promover os seus produtos junto de um vasto público. Ofereça um apoio ao cliente de qualidade, trate rapidamente as devoluções ou os problemas dos clientes e esforce-se constantemente por melhorar a experiência geral de compra na sua loja virtual. Ao combinar uma loja virtual bem concebida com uma estratégia de marketing eficaz e um serviço ao cliente excecional, pode maximizar as suas vendas de dropshipping e construir um negócio de comércio eletrónico de sucesso. Identificar os tipos de conteúdos rentáveis é essencial para os criadores de conteúdos em linha que procuram maximizar as suas receitas. Diferentes formatos de conteúdo podem ser rentabilizados de diferentes formas e é crucial compreender que tipos de conteúdo são mais rentáveis num determinado contexto. As parcerias com marcas para promover os seus produtos ou serviços em vídeos podem gerar receitas significativas através de colaborações pagas. As publicações nas redes sociais também podem ser uma importante fonte de receitas em linha. O Instagram, o TikTok ou o YouTube podem trabalhar com marcas para criar conteúdos patrocinados ou promover produtos junto do seu público. Estas parcerias pagas podem ser extremamente lucrativas para os criadores com uma base de subscritores empenhada. Além disso, a cr ação e a venda de produtos digitais, como livros electrónicos, cursos em linha ou modelos gráficos, podem constituir uma fonte estável de receitas em linha. Os criadores talentosos podem rentabilizar a sua experiência oferecendo conteúdos exclusivos a um público disposto a pagar pelo acesso a estes recursos especializados. Por último, o marketing de afiliados é outra estratégia popular para gerar receitas em linha através de conteúdos. Ao recomendarem produtos ou serviços de terceiros através de ligações de afi iados, os criadores podem ganhar comissões por cada venda efectuada em resultado da sua recomendação. Esta abordagem pode ser particularmente lucrativa se o criador tiver um público fiel e empenhado pronto a seguir as suas recomendações. Em conclusão, a identificação dos tipos de conteúdo que geram receitas em linha requer um conhecimento profundo do mercado e do público-alvo. A criação de conteúdos de qualidade é a chave para atrair e reter um público-alvo. Para o fazer, é crucial compreender as necessidades, os interesses e as preferências do seu público, a fim de produzir conteúdos relevantes e cativantes. Uma abordagem eficaz é efetuar uma análise aprofundada do seu público para identificar os assuntos que geram mais interesse. Utilizando ferramentas de análise das redes sociais ou inquéritos, pode recolher dados valiosos sobre as preferências do seu público e adaptar o seu conteúdo em conformidade. Além disso, diversificar o formato do conteúdo pode ajudar a atrair uma vasta gama de públicos. Ao manter uma cadência regular e previsível, pode fidelizar o público, fornecendo-lhe um fluxo constante de novas informações e aumentando a sua confiança na sua marca. Por último, não se esqueça da importância da interação com o seu público. Em conclusão, a criação de conteúdos de qualidade que atraiam o seu público-alvo requer uma compreensão profunda das suas necessidades e preferências. Ao adaptar a sua estratégia editorial de acordo com o feedback do seu público e ao encorajar a interação e o envolvimento, pode maximizar o impacto do seu conteúdo e aumentar a sua rentabilidade a longo prazo.

Rentabilizar os conteúdos através de publicidade, parcerias e produtos digitais

Quando se trata de rentabilizar o seu conteúdo, existem várias estratégias eficazes que o podem ajudar a gerar receitas e, ao mesmo tempo, oferecer valor acrescentado ao seu público. Pode incorporar anúncios no seu sítio Web, vídeos ou podcasts para chegar a um público vasto e ser pago com base no número de visualizações ou cliques. É essencial escolher anunciantes que sejam relevantes para o seu público, a fim de maximizar os seus ganhos e manter os seus subscritores envolvidos. As parcerias com outras marcas ou influenciadores também podem ser uma fonte de rendimento interessante. Ao colaborar com empresas com ideias semelhantes, pode criar conteúdos patrocinados ou promoções cruzadas que beneficiam tanto o seu público como os seus parceiros. Certifique-se de que estas colaborações são transparentes e autênticas para manter a confiança do seu público. Por último, a criação e venda de produtos digitais pode ser outra fonte de rendimento sustentável. Quer se trate de livros electrónicos, cursos em linha, ferramentas digitais ou mesmo de subscrições premium, a oferta de conteúdos exclusivos com elevado valor acrescentado pode incentivar o seu público a investir nos seus produtos. Combinando judiciosamente publicidade, parcerias e produtos digitais, pode diversificar as suas fontes de rendimento, oferecendo simultaneamente conteúdos enriquecedores e relevantes ao seu público-alvo. Quando se trata de gerir eficazmente o tempo e os recursos em linha, o planeamento das actividades desempenha um papel crucial na maximização da produtividade. Ao estabelecer um calendário claro e estruturado, as pessoas podem organizar as suas tarefas para otimizar a sua eficiência. A utilização de ferramentas de gestão do tempo em linha também pode ser benéfica para um planeamento eficaz. Em conclusão, o planeamento rigoroso e metódico das suas actividades em linha é um fator essencial para maximizar a sua produtividade.

Utilizar ferramentas e técnicas para otimizar o tempo e os recursos

Quando se trata de otimizar o seu tempo e recursos, a utilização das ferramentas e técnicas certas pode facilitar muito a gestão eficaz das suas actividades.

Utilizar aplicações de gestão do tempo: Aplicações como

Trello, Asana, Todoist e Google Calendar oferecem uma série de funcionalidades para organizar tarefas, definir prazos, partilhar projectos em equipa e acompanhar o progresso em tempo real. Do mesmo modo, o método Eisenhower, que consiste em classificar as tarefas de acordo com a sua urgência e importância, ajuda-o a organizar melhor a sua agenda, concentrando-se nas actividades essenciais. O recurso a um assistente virtual ou a delegação de responsabilidades pode libertar tempo para se concentrar nas actividades essenciais que requerem atenção. Estas ferramentas e técnicas são úteis não só para gerir o tempo, mas também para otimizar a utilização dos recursos disponíveis. Quando se trata de gerir eficazmente o tempo e os recursos em linha, é crucial evitar certas armadilhas comuns que podem prejudicar a produtividade e o sucesso. Ao identificar estes potenciais obstáculos, é possível contorná-los e melhorar significativamente a gestão do tempo e dos recursos. É essencial definir objectivos claros e limitar o consumo de informações irrelevantes para se concentrar nas tarefas prioritárias. É aconselhável definir períodos dedicados sem interrupções para que se possa concentrar totalmente nas tarefas importantes. É essencial escolher as aplicações correctas para as suas necessidades específicas e não se deixar dominar por uma multiplicidade de ferramentas inúteis que complicam em vez de ajudar. Ao evitar estas armadilhas comuns da gestão do tempo e dos recursos em linha, pode maximizar a sua eficiência e produtividade.

Reservar a otimização da produtividade www.exemple.com/productivite-outils-numeriques com ferramentas.

Perseverança e criatividade para ter sucesso em

O sucesso online depende não só das competências técnicas, mas também de uma mentalidade positiva e perseverante. A definição de objectivos claros e exequíveis é a chave para ultrapassar os obstáculos. A perseverança desempenha um papel crucial na realização dos objectivos em linha. A capacidade de persistir nos seus esforços, de se adaptar à mudança e de enfrentar os desafios com determinação são qualidades essenciais para o sucesso em linha. Em vez de se deixar desencorajar pelas dificuldades encontradas, é necessário adotar uma abordagem construtiva, procurando soluções alternativas e mantendo-se aberto às mudanças necessárias para progredir em direção aos seus objectivos. Em conclusão, cultivar uma mentalidade de sucesso e ultrapassar os obstáculos é fundamental para o sucesso em linha.

Encontrar soluções criativas para se destacar num mercado competitivo

Num ambiente online saturado e competitivo, é essencial encontrar formas criativas de se destacar e atrair a atenção de potenciais clientes.

Ao utilizar as redes sociais de forma original, ao lançar campanhas virais ou ao oferecer conteúdos envolventes e divertidos, uma empresa pode despertar o interesse e o empenho da sua comunidade em linha. Em conclusão, encontrar soluções criativas para se destacar num mercado competitivo é essencial para o sucesso online. Ao cultivar um espírito de inovação e explorar constantemente novas ideias e abordagens, uma empresa pode não só sobreviver num ambiente competitivo, mas também prosperar e crescer de forma sustentável em linha.

Adaptar-se à mudança e aproveitar as oportunidades para continuar a gerar receitas

A capacidade de adaptação às rápidas mudanças no mercado em linha é crucial para manter a viabilidade de uma empresa e continuar a gerar receitas. Uma estratégia eficaz para se adaptar à mudança é manter-se atento às tendências do mercado, ao comportamento dos consumidores e aos desenvolvimentos tecnológicos. Ao manter-se constantemente informada, uma empresa pode antecipar futuras mudanças e ajustar a sua estratégia em conformidade.

Por exemplo, se uma nova plataforma de redes sociais ganhar popularidade, a empresa deve estar preparada para investir tempo e recursos para atingir um novo público. Em conclusão, a adaptação à mudança e o aproveitamento das oportunidades são fundamentais para manter a competitividade e a rentabilidade de um negócio em linha.

Como se adaptar às rápidas mudanças no mercado online. Estratégias de crescimento para as empresas em linha. Revista internacional de gestão e economia.

How to make $1,000 a day online é um recurso inestimável para quem procura gerar rendimentos online de forma eficaz. O autor explora em profundidade as estratégias, ferramentas e técnicas necessárias para atingir este objetivo ambicioso.

Através de uma análise aprofundada do mercado online, este livro oferece uma perspetiva única sobre as oportunidades lucrativas que existem na Internet. Seja através de marketing de afiliados, dropshipping, criação de conteúdos ou outros meios, o autor guia o leitor através dos passos essenciais para iniciar e desenvolver um negócio online lucrativo. Com ênfase na perseverança, criatividade e gestão eficaz do tempo e dos recursos, "Como ganhar 1000 dólares por dia na Internet" oferece um plano de ação concreto para quem quer transformar a sua presença online numa fonte de rendimento estável e significativa.

How to make $1,000 a day online" is an invaluable resource for those looking to generate income online effectively. The author explores in depth the strategies, tools and techniques needed to achieve this ambitious goal.

Based on a systematic approach and in-depth research, the author presents valuable information and practical advice on how to maximise your earnings on the Internet. Case studies, expert testimonials and detailed analyses are used to illustrate the different methods available and help readers find the one that suits them best.

Through an in-depth analysis of the online marketplace, this book offers a unique perspective on the lucrative opportunities that exist on the internet. Whether through affiliate marketing, dropshipping, content creation or other means, the author guides the reader through the essential steps to starting and developing a profitable online business.

With its emphasis on perseverance, creativity and effective management of time and resources, "How to earn $1,000 a day on the Internet" offers a concrete action plan for those who want to transform their online presence into a stable and significant source of income.

This book is an essential guide for anyone who wants to succeed in today's digital economy. It offers not only practical knowledge but also an invitation to take your financial destiny into your own hands through the limitless possibilities offered by the internet.

yes

I want morebooks!

Buy your books fast and straightforward online - at one of world's fastest growing online book stores! Environmentally sound due to Print-on-Demand technologies.

Buy your books online at
www.morebooks.shop

Compre os seus livros mais rápido e diretamente na internet, em uma das livrarias on-line com o maior crescimento no mundo! Produção que protege o meio ambiente através das tecnologias de impressão sob demanda.

Compre os seus livros on-line em
www.morebooks.shop

Printed by Books on Demand GmbH, Norderstedt / Germany